LIVING THE
CATHOLIC
FAITH

LIVING THE CATHOLIC *FAITH*

Rediscovering the Basics

CHARLES J. CHAPUT, O.F.M. Cap.

CHARIS

SERVANT PUBLICATIONS
ANN ARBOR, MICHIGAN

Charis Books is an imprint of Servant Publications designed to serve Roman
Catholics.

All Scripture quotations, unless otherwise indicated, are taken from the Revised
Standard Version of the Bible, copyright 1946, 1952, 1971 by the Division of
Christian Education of the National Council of Churches of Christ in the USA.
Used by permission.

Excerpts from the English translation of the *Catechism of the Catholic Church* for
use in the United States of America. Copyright © 1994, United States Catholic
Conference, Inc.—Libreria Editrice Vaticana. Used with Permission.

Published by Servant Publications
P.O. Box 8617
Ann Arbor, Michigan 48107

01   02   03   04   10   9   8   7   6   5   4   3

Printed in the United States of America
ISBN 0-56955-191-X

LIBRARY OF CONGRESS CATALOGING-IN-PUBLICATION DATA

Chaput, Charles J.
    Living the Catholic faith: a return to the basics / Charles J. Chaput.
        p. cm.
    ISBN 1-56955-191-X (alk. paper)
    1. Christian life—Catholic authors. 2. Spiritual life—Catholic Church.
3. Catholic Church—Doctrines. I. Title.
BX2350.3 .C43 2001
248.4'82—dc21

                                                    00-065664

To my mother, Marian, and my father, Joseph,
who by living Jesus Christ in their own lives
gave me the gifts of life, love, and faith

"He knew now that, at the end, there was only one thing that counted—to be a saint."

The Power and the Glory
Graham Greene

Contents

Foreword

Ideas are always easier in the thinking than in the doing, and this book proves the point. The idea behind these pages was to help people understand their Catholic faith a little more clearly, and to live it a little more eagerly. Faith for me is like oxygen: I can't imagine a world without it. The presence of Jesus Christ in the lives of my family and friends, and in my own life, gives meaning to everything else. Yet, experiencing that and arguing it persuasively are two very different things. Therefore, these pages don't claim to be comprehensive. Others have offered a more complete and engaging explanation of our faith, and looking back over a text, one always finds so much more that can be said—or at least said better.

Still, if this book helps one person to encounter the Lord, or to deepen a love for the Church, then it succeeds. God made us to be saints, and since we're created for heaven, the very least we can do is *try* to cooperate with God in getting us there. As Teresa of Avila once said, "In the measure you desire Him, you will find Him."

Even a modest book like this owes much to many friends. Bert Ghezzi of Servant Publications first suggested the idea, and supported and encouraged it throughout. Doug Bushman and Anthony Lilles provided early help. Bob Lockwood's talent and dedication were invaluable in editing the material. Bill Beckman, Marco Roman, and Christopher West all reviewed the text and made important contributions.

Above all, my thanks go to the people, priests, religious, deacons, and seminarians of the Church in northern Colorado, many of whom experienced these chapters in their original Jubilee Lecture format and asked questions that clearly improved the text.

Finally, a special and grateful nod to Kerry Kober and Fran Maier of my personal staff—my co-conspirators in this effort from the beginning.

+cjc
Solemnity of All Saints
November 1, 2000

CHAPTER ONE

Becoming a Christian

Have you ever been to Niagara Falls? If not, try to imagine them. If you have, close your eyes and remember. What's the most overwhelming thing about Niagara Falls?

It's the sound. You can *hear* the Falls from miles away. At first, the noise is just a steady background rumble. Yet it builds and builds until, at the brink, the thunder can almost paralyze. At the brink, the ground vibrates. For anyone gazing out across the curtain of white and turbulent water, the Falls are a lesson in humility. Human beings have done amazing things in our lifetime. But the Falls are God's architecture—God's engineering—cut right into the raw granite of the earth. All the water in Lakes Superior, Huron, Michigan, and Erie sooner or later goes over the edge. That's a lot of water. It's cold, fast, and powerful, and it doesn't care what—or who—it takes with it.

People have been going over the Falls for a long time. Some intend to, and some don't. The people who deliberately shoot the Falls build very strong barrels or cylinders to protect themselves from the rocks, the water, and the impact of falling 163 feet. To have any chance of surviving, they need to hit exactly the right channel in the current. That channel needs to drop them exactly into the one small pool at the base of the Canadian Falls that has no rocks. And then they have to be lucky enough to avoid getting trapped behind the wall of falling water, or they'll run out of air. Even under the best circumstances, with the best preparation, it's a very risky stunt, which is why it's also illegal. In other words, the Falls are very beautiful and very dangerous at the same time. This leads to my story.

It happened maybe forty years ago. An uncle took his young niece and nephew out on the Niagara River in his powerboat, a few miles above the Falls. This is common in the summer, because the current is fairly gentle at that point and the Coast Guard patrols the area. This time the engine failed. The man didn't have a radio. The Coast Guard didn't spot him until the boat was already in the grip of the river. Hundreds of people saw what was happening. They ran to the shore, but of course they couldn't help. The man had only two life jackets. He gave them to the children. A few hundred yards above the brink, the boat hit a rock and overturned. The uncle disappeared in the water. The boy was swept over the edge but, purely by God's grace, he hit just the right channel. That channel dropped him at the only possible place—at exactly the right angle and speed—so he could survive the plunge. He is still the only person to go over Niagara Falls unprotected, and live.

Yet my story really concerns the young girl. She was trapped in a different channel and banged around on the rocks. Then she shot toward the brink like a bullet, just beyond the reach of the crowd. That should have been the end of her, except that twenty yards from the brink, a man jumped into the river. While he held on to a friend with one hand, he grabbed the girl with his other hand, just as she swept past. Then he hung on to her until the people on the bank could pull them both to safety. The water at that point is chest-deep, moving very fast, and ice-cold. The riverbed is as slippery as greased glass. But he did it anyway, and he saved her life.

Now that's a true story. And if you want a hint of what "becoming a Christian" is about, and why it's important, there's no better place to start. Each of us is that girl. We're all swept along, beaten up, and paralyzed by a river of sin—our own sins, and the world's sinfulness, flowing down all the way from Adam and Eve. It's the river we call original sin. In the grip of that river, we can see our own deaths just over the brink. Yet no matter how strong a swimmer we may be, no matter how hard we may struggle, we can't do anything about it on our own. We can't save ourselves. Then a Savior jumps into the current, for no reason other than wanting to rescue us. And He pulls us to safety.

That's the nature of Baptism. Becoming a Christian begins in Baptism, with God intervening to save us. It's His free gift and His initiative. That's why Baptism is not just a pious family social event. It's literally a matter of life and death. Eternity hinges on it. Jesus said, unless a man be "born of water and the Spirit, he cannot enter the kingdom of God" (Jn 3:5). The reason is simple. We're born loved by God, but also estranged from Him. We're born into that river of sin, and we are part of it. In Baptism, God pulls us out of the river and saves us from the ruin that lies just over the brink.

"Sin" is a bad word these days. Not because we don't believe in it, but because *we don't want to believe in it.* We live in an age when we spend billions of dollars every year delaying death, denying age, and explaining away sin. Yet we can't evade any of these things. Something's wrong with the fabric of our lives, and we can all instinctively sense it. There's a dissonance in our own hearts, and a disharmony in the world around us, that psychology and affluence can't fix.

It's what the poet William Butler Yeats meant—without intending it—when he wrote that, "things fall apart, the center cannot hold." God is the glue to human meaning. When we turn away from Him in sin, the center cannot hold because the glue is gone. The result is suffering. History may have seen unhappier times, but the twentieth century was surely bloody enough for any generation, and the wounds are everywhere. You may have heard the music of Don Henley. He has a strange and arresting song on one of his albums called *The Garden of Allah.* In it, the devil comes to modern Los Angeles to do his wicked work. Yet in the course of the song, the devil discovers that the city reminds him too much of home. All his work is already done, so he leaves, disappointed by his own success.

Sin is real, and not only in Los Angeles, but in each city, home, and heart. It leads to division and death. We can deny it only by living a kind of schizophrenia, which is exactly what our culture is trying to do. I doubt that I need to convince you of that. You can see for yourself, just by surfing your television channels or skimming the daily newspaper headlines. If Baptism isn't equally real—if it's just a nice metaphor or a Church word for dealing with the flaws in our gene code; if it doesn't truly deliver us from sin—then our faith is worthless, and we have better things to do than delude ourselves.

The power of Baptism *is* real. The delusion in our world isn't faith, but the lack of it. Convincing ourselves that we're not really in the river won't suspend gravity when we go over the falls. We find the proof of Baptism's power not just in the revealed Word of God but in the sacrament's effect on individuals, and on the life of the believing community. Despite all of our own mistakes, and all of the world's persecution, the faith still lives and grows. Holiness happens. Saints happen. Where evil exists, grace abounds more so, if we just have the eyes to see it. Baptism plants a very tenacious seed, which is cultivated to full life by the Church.

This brings me back to the little girl rescued from the Niagara River. Two things happened to that girl. The first is obvious. She was saved from death. Yet there's more. *She was also delivered into a new life*, a life she had no reason to expect, and which was changed permanently by her brush with death. The similarity to Baptism is this: Baptism not only delivers us from death, it also delivers us into a new life, into a "community of life"—the Church. The Church grows, nourishes, reinforces, and deepens our relationship with God, the Author of life itself. Being saved from death is a pretty good deal. Yet, in a sense, the really interesting part, the really important part, is what we do with life afterward.

God has an opinion about that. He saves us for a purpose. That purpose is love. He loves each of us infinitely and ardently, as a bridegroom loves his bride. He loves us enough to share with us the mission of His Son, Jesus, the task of redeeming and sanctifying the world, and drawing all souls into His friendship. That's why Christian love is never a passive verb. It's always active.

Of course, before we act on God's love, we first must receive it and allow it to transform us. As Mary shows us, "let it be done unto me" comes before "let me do it." Yet, having received the gift of faith in Baptism, we can then respond to Jesus Christ when He sends us to "make disciples of all nations," just as He Himself was sent by His Father. Baptism always implies two things: communion in and with the Church; and mission to the world. This means that each of us is a missionary, and we need to act like it.

Becoming a Christian is never *merely* an act of loyalty to an institution, or agreeing with a body of doctrines. Of course, these things are very important. Vatican II reminded Catholics that no distinction can exist between the so-called institutional Church and the body of Christ. We can't claim to be part of the People of God, but separate ourselves from the structures of authority in the Church. Church structure is part of the apostolic reality. It's the bone and muscle of the body of Christ.

In like manner, doctrines are vitally important because they organize, clarify, and ensure the proper transmission of God's truth. Around that truth we build our lives in Christ. Knowing the teachings of the Church and living them in a spirit of love and obedience should be the natural instinct of every believer. Why? Because the Church teaches the truth, and the truth makes us free; in fact, the teaching of the Church is the teaching of Christ. That's why the idea of "cafeteria Catholics" is such a contradiction. The Catholic who picks and chooses his doctrines sets his own judgment above that of the Church. In doing so, in a certain sense he removes himself from her. Being 80 percent Catholic is like being 80 percent married. It doesn't work.

Having said that, we need to understand that the heart of becoming a Christian is the relationship established with God. Christians preach and believe that God reveals Himself fully, for all people, for all time, in Jesus Christ. The God we see in Jesus Christ anchors our entire understanding of the world. So, what are the defining qualities of that God?

First and above all, God is personal. In fact, He is a communion of loving Persons. God is not an idea, or an ideology, or an equation, or magic, or a force, or an intelligent gas cloud, or a hypothesis. God is as real and as personal as you and me— only much more so, because God is the source of personhood and the author of reality. We can love a person and, being personal, God can love us back. We can't love a gas cloud, and ideas don't have relationships.

Second, God is not only just but also loving and forgiving. He judges and condemns sin, but He also sent His Son to die and then rise for us in order to deliver us from judgment. He did it because He loves us. He continues to love the world enough to invite us to cooperate in its redemption.

Third, He has a plan for us. The Father of Jesus Christ is not the clockmaker god of the Enlightenment. He doesn't wind up the universe, then walk away to study it from a distance. He's not only transcendent but also immanent. He's not just out there in the Milky Way but down here in the flesh and blood of the world. He's involved. "The Word became flesh and dwelt among us" (Jn 1:14). God knows us, because in Jesus He's one of us.

That's why Jesus not only reveals to us the nature of God, but the nature of the human person as well. If God is willing to become a man and suffer and die for us, then we're worth something infinitely valuable. God loves us because He sees us as He intended us to be: children of beauty, light, and truth. God doesn't make junk. He doesn't make losers. Yes, our sins are very real. We're responsible for our own actions. Yet they don't subtract anything from God's love for us.

The word "responsible" is important because it reveals another key truth about the human person. We are responsible *because we are free*. We are not just determined by economic forces and scientific laws. Our choices are real. They have meaning. Mary could have said "no" to the Holy Spirit. God loves us ardently and wants us to love Him in return, but the irony of love is that it requires freedom. Saying "yes" to God means something only if we can also say "no." Jesus is the model of human freedom, the man who knows and freely chooses what is right, instead of making other, easier choices. He shows us the tremendous trust and respect God places in us by giving us real freedom. We are loved because, as God's children, we are lovable.

Finally, Jesus also reveals to us our own hunger for God. Jesus doesn't fear His Father, and He doesn't merely "respect" Him. He loves His Father with His whole heart. He calls Him *Abba*, "Dear Father," a term of endearment. That love and hunger resonate deeply in every human heart.

One of my favorite passages in Scripture is Psalm 63:

Oh God, thou art my God, I seek thee; my soul thirsts for
thee;
My flesh faints for thee, as in a dry and weary land where no
water is.
So I have looked upon thee in the sanctuary, beholding thy
power and glory.
Because thy steadfast love is better than life, my lips will praise
thee.
I will bless thee as long as I live;
I will lift up my hands and call on thy name.

Reflect on that language for a moment. Each of the verbs is
rich and active: I seek thee; I will bless thee; my lips will praise
thee; my flesh faints for thee; I will lift up my hands and call on
thy name. This is a real love song. David wrote it in the wilder-
ness of Judah probably three thousand years ago, but it
resonates in the depths of the human heart just as powerfully
today.

To say that God loves man, and man loves God doesn't even
begin to capture what the psalmist means. Psalm 63 is a song of
yearning, longing, thirst, and hunger for God, the way the
bridegroom and bride yearn for each other in the Song of
Songs—mind and heart, body and soul. The heart of becoming
a Christian is giving yourself away to God, possessing Him, and
being possessed by Him. It's why French Catholic writer
François Mauriac said that, "Anyone who has truly known God
can never be cured of Him." It's why Augustine wrote, "Oh
God, our hearts are restless, until they rest in thee."

Faith is a love story. The greatest story ever told.

But *every* real love story is a great love story, and every great love story creates new life. Real love is always fruitful. It is never barren. The love of husbands and wives bears fruit most obviously in the lives of their children, but also in many forms of Christian service and in the witness their love provides to other people. Priests, religious, and people called to the single vocation are just as fruitful, but in a different way. They nourish the Church with their lives. They create a witness of radical service, and a legacy of spiritual children and apostolic works.

The community of faith is very similar to the individuals within it. The Church is the bride of Christ, and that love needs to bear fruit. The "new life" which the Church brings to the world is salvation in Jesus Christ. She does this through preaching, teaching, and living the gospel and celebrating the sacraments.

In the Gospel of Matthew, Jesus tells us, "Go therefore and make disciples of all nations, baptizing them in the name of the Father, and of the Son and of the Holy Spirit" (Mt 28:19). Jesus was talking to us—all of us. When we fail to share our love of Jesus Christ with others, it diminishes in our own hearts. If we don't live that love and share it, we lose it. And we can't be happy without it. That's what St. Paul meant when he wrote, "Woe to me if I do not preach the Gospel!" (1 Cor 9:16).

Who could doubt that the world *needs* the gospel? The Church in the United States finds herself ministering to a culture of light and shadow: on the one hand, millions of people who are young, successful, highly educated, and often unchurched; on the other, millions who are poor, immigrant, elderly, or marginalized. This is mission territory. This is the new Areopagus, the new Greek court, where, similar to the challenge once faced by St. Paul, the faith must be brought alive to a proud and deeply skeptical culture.

This is the kind of environment John Paul II had in mind in 1985, when he spoke to the Pontifical Council for Culture: "You must help the Church respond to [the] fundamental questions for the cultures of today: How is the message of the Church accessible to the new cultures, to contemporary forms of understanding and sensitivity? How can the Church make herself understood by the modern spirit, so proud of its achievements, and at the same time so uneasy for the future of the human family?"

It's what the Pope had in mind when he wrote in *Crossing the Threshold of Hope*: "Against the spirit of the world, the Church takes up anew each day a struggle that is none other *than the struggle for the world's soul.*"

This is our baptismal call to a "new evangelization." A new evangelizing spirit needs to be born in each of our hearts, and if it is, God will use it to win the soul of the world to Jesus Christ. Certainly, as Catholics, we pray for more priests to lead us in this task. There is no gospel witness without the Church; there is no Church without the Eucharist; and there is no Eucharist without the priest. We need more priests, good men who are well formed, men who love Jesus Christ and His people. That's a most urgent step in renewing Christ's Church.

But if it stops there, no matter how many good men we attract to the priesthood, we fail. Ultimately, just as there's no Church without the Eucharist, and no Eucharist without the priest, *there are no priests without families on fire with Christ.* Families who help their sons and daughters hear God's call; who affirm, support, and encourage the priests and religious who already serve them; who live their lives in a way that proves to our priests and religious that their sacrifices make a difference.

So, we need a commitment to what the "new evangelization" really is: a communion and mission of the whole Church, ordained, religious, and lay, each respecting the other, each supporting the other, all serving the Lord by bringing the Good News to the world, and the world to the Good News. *That's* the true equality of the faithful: each unique; each complementing and completing the other; all together in service; and on fire with Jesus Christ. When we finally choose to live out the consequences of our Baptism, God creates a kind of holy restlessness in our midst, and shakes us out of our complacency. Complacency is the enemy of mission; the enemy of the gospel; the enemy of the Christian life.

All of this should lead us back to our knees in prayer—and for me personally, prayer to St. Francis of Assisi. The "new evangelization" echoes with Christ's words to Francis to "repair my house." God will use us—all of us—to renew His house. In fact, Francis may be the model of Church renewal for every age. He lived in a time at least as complicated as our own. Society and the Church were in upheaval. The feudal system was falling apart. For much of his life, Francis was lost in the confusion. Yet in his experience of conversion, he came to some basic insights. Those insights gave him freedom, and enabled him to live the gospel life with simplicity and clarity in such a way that in the process of his own conversion he became a leader of conversion in the Church and society.

The insight of St. Francis was very simple. He experienced

God as a providential Father. Knowing that a father would not give his son a scorpion when he asked for bread, he began to live his faith as a trusting child. Of course, this led to a deepening identification with Christ, the Son in whom we become God's children.

Because of his relationship with God as Father and Jesus Christ as Brother, Francis began to encounter people in a new way. They became his sisters and brothers, not just strangers, because they were sons and daughters of God and sisters and brothers to Jesus Christ. This also explains Francis' profoundly peaceful relationship with creation, because creation, too, flows from the hand of a loving Father.

St. Francis called his brothers to live the gospel with simplicity and honesty. He used the words "without gloss," or *sine glossa*, in his Testament. Francis understood that the gospel wasn't complicated, but it *was* demanding and difficult. The theologians and lawyers of the day had written commentaries. They were called "glosses", and these glosses either explained away the gospel demands, or argued away our responsibility for following the letter of the gospel. Francis wanted none of that. His ability to be a poor man also flowed from his understanding of God's providence. He wanted to be dependent on nothing but the providential care of God.

What's this got to do with us today? The faith of Francis is part of our baptismal inheritance. In Baptism, we are saved from death and given new life. Now, like Francis, it's vital for us to become new women and new men—to put away the conflicts of the past and to give ourselves absolutely to God.

CHAPTER TWO

Living in Christ

And He came to Nazareth, where He had been brought up; and He went to the synagogue, as His custom was, on the Sabbath day. And He stood up to read; and there was given to Him the book of the prophet Isaiah. He opened the book and found the place where it was written,

"The Spirit of the Lord is upon me, because He has anointed me to preach good news to the poor. He has sent me to proclaim release to the captives and recovering of sight to the blind, to set at liberty those who are oppressed, to proclaim the acceptable year of the Lord."

And He closed the book, and gave it back to the attendant, and sat down; and the eyes of all in the synagogue were fixed on Him. And He began to say to them, "Today, this scripture has been fulfilled in your hearing."

LUKE 4:16-21

G od's Word has countless moments of wisdom and exultation, but this is truly one of the most electric passages in the Bible. A philosopher once said that in the presence of the Numinous—and by "Numinous" he meant the mystery and holiness of God—creation vibrates. It sings and overflows. So, too, in these verses from Scripture. The more deeply we pray over this passage from the fourth chapter of Luke, the more electricity we find in it. The heart begins to overflow with the hope that something utterly new begins in these words of Jesus.

Imagine yourself on a bench in that synagogue. Fill your memory with more than a thousand years of Jewish yearning for a Messiah, and hundreds of years of captivity, wandering, struggle, and oppression. Remember the sacredness of God's name, which for Jews was, and is, unspeakable. Imagine an entire people's longing for a deliverer, tied up for generations in the prophecies of Isaiah 61. Now imagine the moment when a familiar young rabbi, a carpenter's son, claims to be the fulfillment of that longing, and then goes on to admonish His listeners for their lack of faith (see Lk 4:22-30).

Only two reasonable responses flow from what Jesus has claimed, and "polite interest" isn't one of them. Jesus is not just a bright young teacher with an ego problem. He's either what He claims to be—the *Christos* in Greek, which means the Anointed One—or a blasphemer.

Everyone in the synagogue quickly understood what Jesus was saying. They also may have sensed its implications for each of their lives. Most were filled with anger. The Revised Standard Version translation of Scripture uses that wonderful biblical word, "wrath," to describe their reaction. Enraged, the townsfolk actually tried to throw Jesus off a cliff. Yet others heard and believed. For them—the weak, the suffering, the lonely, the widowed, the searching—Jesus became God's presence in the world, the living source of joy.

"Joy" is an interesting word. "Contentment" and "happiness" have a kind of restfulness to them. "Joy" has just one syllable, but it's much more active and alive. You may have read *The Screwtape Letters* or some other wonderful book by C.S. Lewis. We remember him as one of the great Christian writers of the twentieth century. Yet he didn't always believe in Jesus Christ. He began his adulthood as a confident and successful atheist intellectual. He had a weakness, though. He was observant, inquisitive, and honest. And he didn't realize until too late that God lurks at the center of every natural virtue. He asked too many questions about people and life, too deeply and too honestly, and he walked right into God's ambush.

God surprised him. In fact, that became the title of Lewis' book about his own conversion: *Surprised by Joy*. At the time, Lewis wrote that, "Really, a young atheist cannot guard his [atheism] too carefully. Dangers lie in wait for him on every side...." He was being humorous, of course, but he also spoke a great truth. Unbelief likes to posture itself as urbane and respectable, but in fact, it's stodgy and sour, because it lacks something fundamental to our nature as humans. Faith has unkempt hair. Faith laughs. *Faith is jubilant* because it connects with the source of all meaning and joy—God Himself.

The wife of one of my more earnest colleagues has a great way of teasing him. She says, "If you're happy, tell your face," and she's got a point. A healthy concern about problems is good. But fretfulness and brooding are foolish. They suggest an absorption with things, and a lack of trust in God's providence. Joy flows naturally from the presence of God. This is why Catholics have always said, "there are no unhappy saints." All saints, finally, are consumed by joy. That's what God intends for each of us, and it's the reason Jesus came. That's the purpose of "living in Christ"—joy in His presence.

Remember those words of Luke 4:16-21. Then recall the first public moments of Karol Wojtyla when he became Pope John Paul II: He said, "Be not afraid." Those were tall words to use in the bloodiest century of human history, but he meant them. Living in Jesus Christ means choosing to trust. It means living without fear. What a remarkable contrast the pope's message of hope offers to the violence of the modern secular world on the one hand, and the anxiety of some fundamentalist groups, on the other.

From very early in his pontificate, John Paul described the Great Jubilee of the Year 2000 as the "hermeneutical key" or the "key to interpreting" his ministry. What did he mean? He meant that understanding the Great Jubilee is the road to understanding not just his pontificate, but also the message he preaches about how we should continue to live as Christians in the decades ahead. And the key to understanding the Great Jubilee is found precisely in Luke 4: "Today, this scripture"—and all Scripture—"has been fulfilled in your hearing."

Faith is jubilant, and the words "jubilant" and "jubilee" are obviously related. Here's the connection. The jubilee has a long tradition in our religious experience. It goes back to the Book of Leviticus in the Old Testament. For ancient Israel, the Sabbath, which fell every seventh day; the sabbatical year, which fell every seventh year; and the jubilee, which Jews celebrated every fifty years, all had a similar goal. They all sought to recover the joy of God's presence and to draw the Chosen People closer to God by dedicating time exclusively to Him. In the jubilee year, debts were forgiven, slaves were freed, and the land lay fallow. When lived sincerely, the jubilee resulted in a rebirth of justice among God's people by wiping the slate clean. It created peace between people through a radical dependence on God, which everyone shared. God would reward Israel's trust with the abundance of His providence and joy.

In our reading from Luke 4, Jesus declares Himself as the fulfillment of Isaiah's prophecy. He is the "fullness of time." He is God's joy and truth incarnate. In Him, the prophesied "year of the Lord's favor" begins. In Him, the year of favor never ends. Even His name proclaims salvation. Jesus is *Yeshua* in Hebrew, which means "God saves." Jesus is the center and meaning of history, precisely because He is the salvation of the world. As John Paul wrote in his 1994 apostolic letter, *As the Third Millennium Draws Near*, "In Jesus Christ, the Word made flesh, time becomes a dimension of God, who is Himself eternal" (10).

This is why "living in Christ" can never include living in fear. It's no accident that the *Pastoral Constitution on the Church in the Modern World*—arguably the most moving document of the Second Vatican Council—is entitled *Gaudium et Spes*, which in Latin means "joy and hope." And it's no accident that Pope John Paul II, who took an active role in the council from beginning to end, would write in *Crossing the Threshold of Hope* that, "Gospel means 'good news,' and the Good News is always an invitation to joy."

John Paul continues, "[The Gospel] is a grand affirmation of the world and of man, because it is the revelation of the truth about God. God is the primary source of joy and hope for man. This is the God whom Christ revealed; God who is Creator and

Father; God 'who so loved the world that He gave His only Son, so that everyone who believes in Him might not perish but might have eternal life' (see Jn 3:16)." And he adds, "The Gospel, above all else, is the *joy of creation* [which is completed, in turn,] by the *joy of salvation*, by the *joy of redemption*." In Jesus Christ, "The Creator of man is also his Redeemer ... [and] good is greater than all that is evil in the world."

How do we "live in Christ" in practical terms? As we've seen, *becoming* a Christian happens on God's terms. The initiative belongs to Him, not us. We can long for God and search for God, and we can cooperate with the gift of faith when it comes, but we don't really "find God." God finds us. God reveals Himself to us, not the other way around. Without Him, we don't even have the vocabulary to pose the "God question."

At the same time, because we have a God-given free will, we can reject God when He comes to us. That freedom suits God's purpose very well. Being a God of love, He wants to be loved freely in return. The Creator of the universe asks permission of Mary to send her His Son. So it is with each of us. God invites us, courts us, and draws us close to Him. Yet He will not force His love on an unwilling soul.

Becoming a Christian, then, is a process that is simultaneously the same and different for everyone. It is the same, in that each person is offered the gift of faith. Then, like Mary, we can each freely choose to accept or reject God's presence. Yet it's also different, because each of us is unique, with a unique personality and temperament, and with unique strengths and weaknesses. The love story between God and each one of us is unique and unrepeatable.

For those who do choose to accept God's love, however, three things are required. We need *conversion,* which means turning away from our sins and toward God; *discipleship,* which means deciding to obey God by following Jesus Christ in everything we do; and *transformation,* which means allowing the Holy Spirit to make us new creatures. We become God's sons and daughters in and through God's Son. All three of these movements in our hearts—conversion, discipleship, and transformation—are *continuous throughout a Christian's life.* They never stop. Scripture says the just man sins seven times a day. Most of the people I know—myself first of all—probably sin a lot more than that. So the task of identifying the sins in our lives and rooting them out with God's help never ends. Conversion can always go deeper. The same is true with discipleship and transformation. We can always do more as apostles, and our transformation is never complete until we fully possess God—and are fully possessed by God—in the life to come.

In all of this, Jesus is the heart of the matter. In the final telling, what makes us Christian is our daily relationship with the living person of Jesus Christ. Christianity is not merely a set of doctrines, though these are essential. Nor is it a body of law or knowledge, tradition, or sentiment, though all of these play a vital role in the life of faith. Christianity is a matter of becoming more like Christ, of becoming daily more configured to the person of Jesus. In Jesus, God adopts us as sons and daughters into His own family of love—the Trinity—where we share in God's own divine life, which is dynamic and eternal.

How do we acquire and deepen that new life in Jesus Christ, when we are born in sin and therefore estranged from God?

God provides us the means to new life in the sacraments, especially in the Sacraments of Initiation, which we know as Baptism, Confirmation, and the Eucharist.

What is a sacrament? In a simple and general sense, a sacrament is something we see, which points to something we cannot see. It's a sign of something else, something greater. For example, all creation is fundamentally sacramental because it points to its Creator, in the same way a Van Gogh painting unmistakably suggests the artist. Psalm 19 says, "The heavens are telling the glory of God, and the firmament proclaims His handiwork." Christian faith is *incarnational*. The Word became flesh. God became man. Christianity understands that human beings are both material and spiritual, and that physical things can point the believer to spiritual realities.

In that sense, Jesus Himself is the first and greatest sacrament. He is the ultimate sign of God's love. In Him, the invisible God is made visible. In the face of Jesus, we see the face of God. The Church is also a sacrament. The Church is a sign of Christ's living presence among us and of His ongoing desire to save us. The seven formal sacraments we learned in grade school—Baptism, Penance, the Eucharist, Confirmation, Matrimony, Holy Orders, and Anointing of the Sick—give concrete expression to the Church's continuation of Christ's saving work in the world.

Let's reflect on that for a moment. Those of us who grew up in the 1950s will probably remember the Baltimore Catechism's definition of a sacrament: A sacrament is "an outward sign, instituted by Christ, to give grace." That's still a good thumbnail description, and many of us can repeat it quite easily from memory. But do we really understand what it means?

When I have the privilege of visiting a parish for the celebration of the Sacrament of Confirmation, I always look for a young girl with several rings on her fingers. A person like that is easy to find these days. I ask her to come forward and visit with me about the meaning of those rings. I ask her, "What does this or that particular ring mean?" She usually responds with either silence or confusion, because it seems like an odd question. It's just a ring—what *could* it mean?

So then I ask, "Well, who gave you the ring?" She'll answer, well, my boyfriend or my mother. Then I ask, "But why did your boyfriend or your mother give it to you, and not to me?" And she laughs, generally with some embarrassment, because the answer of course is that her parent or her boyfriend loves her. And I say, "That's exactly what the ring means. A ring given to us as a gift is an outward sign of something we can't see— love. We know love is real. It's more real than many things we can see very clearly. We can't see love with our eyes, but we know it's real. So a ring is an outward sign of an invisible reality. An outward sign instituted by the person who gave it to us, to show us that person's love." In the same way, the seven sacraments are things we can see—things that have been instituted, or given to us, by Jesus Christ. Through them, He gives us something we *can't* see, which is an embrace of His love.

Since the Second Vatican Council, we've come to talk about the seven sacraments as encounters with Christ. The sacraments are not encounters from a distance, but personal encounters, up close, where Christ comes to us in love, to embrace our lives and to draw us into the life of the Trinity. We need to remember three things in understanding the sacraments correctly.

First, Jesus Himself instituted the seven sacraments. The sacraments were not "invented" by the Church. Yet that doesn't mean Jesus established each of the sacraments in its exact and current form. Jesus founded His Church, died on the cross, and rose from the dead for her. He left her with the authority to carry on His mission. He willed that the life-giving effects of His Passion, death, and resurrection should be offered to all persons, in all times. Just as He touched people's lives in tangible, sacramental ways during His earthly ministry, He now wants His Church to do the same. The Church, following His example and mandate, continues Christ's saving work through sacramental signs. Obviously, these rites have been adapted and reformed over the years so that people of different periods and cultures can more easily receive God's grace. But the seven sacraments are rooted in the will and ministry of the Lord Himself.

Second, the sacraments do indeed "give grace." Yet grace isn't a quantifiable product, like gas at a Texaco station. Grace is a matter of relationship with God. The sacraments give grace by deepening our relationship with Jesus Christ. They do that by providing the means for a divine-human encounter and divine-human cooperation. We "increase in grace" as God deepens His relationship with us. The sacraments offer us the means for that deepening.

Third, the seven sacraments are signs, but they are not *just* signs. They're much more than mere symbols. Each sacrament is an action of Christ Himself, an extension of His paschal mystery. Jesus Christ Himself, the High Priest, touches and transforms us in the water of Baptism, the oil of Confirmation, and the wine and bread of the Eucharist, thereby effecting, or really bringing about, what the sacrament signifies. In Baptism we literally die with Christ and rise with Him to become a new creation. The waters of Baptism wash us clean from sin, save us from spiritual death, and establish our friendship with God. They also carry us into a new community of life, and that new life has big implications. If we're dead to sin, we need to act like it. Baptism initiates us into the two great commissions that Jesus gave to all His followers: to love one another as He loved the Church; and to go and teach all nations in the name of the Father, the Son, and the Holy Spirit. Baptism commissions us into a story—and also into a history.

Again, Christianity is not merely a set of principles or a philosophy of life. Rather, what happens in Baptism is that we're inducted into the history of salvation. It's a story that begins with Genesis and reaches its fulfillment in the passion, death, and resurrection of Jesus of Nazareth. Through our Baptism, we're inserted into this story as key players, and that's infinitely more exciting than receiving a set of principles or a theory. Our obligation through Baptism is to live out the story as God guides us in our time. Being part of that story—the history of salvation—is not just "intellectually satisfying." It's exhilarating to mind, body, and spirit.

The Sacrament of Confirmation seals that baptismal covenant and brings it to fruition. It consecrates us for God's service. It opens our hearts to the Holy Spirit and turns the individual who is saved by Baptism outward with a concern for the salvation of the world. Confirmation is the sacrament of

Pentecost, of Christian witness, enthusiasm, courage, and mission. Lived fully, Confirmation is a sacrament that leaves us permanently hungry for God and permanently eager to "struggle for the soul of the contemporary world."

The Eucharist is the nourishment that sustains us in the journey of life. In the Eucharist, Jesus invites us to offer ourselves with Him, as He offers Himself to the Father—"a pure and holy sacrifice," acceptable to God. The Second Vatican Council described this sacrament as the "source and summit" of the Christian life. The reason is simple and powerful. The Eucharist is where we most vividly encounter Jesus Christ, not as a memory, but as living flesh and blood. The bread and wine of the Eucharist don't "symbolize" God. They become God's body and blood. Therefore, the surest way to an ardent relationship with Jesus Christ is the habit of daily Mass, allowing Him to equip us for whatever each new day brings.

In Deuteronomy 30, God speaks to the Chosen People He loves: "I have set before you life and death, blessing and curse; therefore choose life, that you and your descendants may live...."

More than a thousand years later, in the fullness of time, Jesus of Nazareth said, "I am the way, and the truth, and the life" (Jn 14:6), and "he who eats my flesh and drinks my blood has eternal life" (Jn 6:54). Living in Jesus Christ is the answer to God's invitation in Deuteronomy. Living in Christ is choosing life, because Jesus is not just the source of our joy. He is the one and only way to the fullness of life.

CHAPTER THREE

Growing in Christ

Let's look at two very different readings:

And as [Jesus] was setting out on his journey, a man ran up and knelt before him, and asked him, "Good Teacher, what must I do to inherit eternal life?" And Jesus said to him, "Why do you call me good? No one is good but God alone. You know the commandments: Do not kill. Do not commit adultery. Do not steal. Do not bear false witness. Do not defraud. Honor your father and mother."

And he said to [Jesus], "Teacher, all these I have observed from my youth." And Jesus, looking upon him, loved him, and said to him: "You lack one thing: Go, sell what you have, give to the poor, and you will have treasure in heaven; and come follow me."

And then a second passage:

We believe that we live in the "age of information," that there has been an information "explosion," an information "revolution." While in a certain narrow sense, this is the case, in many important ways, just the opposite is true. We also live at a moment of deep ignorance, when vital knowledge that humans have always possessed about who we are and where we live seems beyond our reach. An Unenlightenment. An age of missing information.

The first reading, of course, is from Scripture, the Gospel of Mark, chapter 10. The second is much more recent. Bill McKibben published it in 1992 in a little book called *The Age of Missing Information*. As research, he arranged, with the help of friends, to videotape every minute, on every television channel, in a single twenty-four-hour period in the Fairfax, Virginia, cable system. That's one full, nonstop day of television on ninety-two different channels. It adds up to 132,480 minutes. McKibben spent the next ten months watching every one of those minutes. Then he spent a similar twenty-four-hour period alone, in silence, in the woods. After that he wrote his book, comparing the two experiences and the information each contained.

You probably know where this is leading. The silence in the forest was fertile with smells and color, memories, thoughts, feelings, and the beauty of nature. The television wasn't. The twenty-two hundred hours of videotape contained a huge amount of information. Some was interesting. Some was urgent. But most—the overwhelming majority of it—was useless. The really important information was missing. And the *really* important question wasn't even asked: "Good Teacher, what must I do to inherit eternal life?"

Let's take it a step further. A couple of years ago, still another very interesting book appeared, called *The Elegant Universe*. It was written for typical, "nonscientist" people, and it had the following premise. Einstein's Relativity physics can explain the behavior of very big cosmic events with great accuracy. Quantum physics can predict behavior on the very small, subatomic level with great accuracy. Yet there's one big problem. They are incompatible theories. They both work, but they seem to contradict each other.

For a scientist, this is rather alarming. So, in *The Elegant Universe*, the author examined another theory that ties these two kinds of physics together. The new theory is called "string theory." String theory, without simplifying it too radically, suggests that the basic "stuff" of creation is strings. These subatomic strings vibrate in ways that create what we *perceive* as particles, waves, or forces.

Here's my point. For you and me and 95 percent of the world's population, *The Elegant Universe*—despite all its astonishing scholarship and ingenuity—never asks the truly important questions: Who made the string, and what does He want from me?

We live in an age of missing information. The most important information seems to be absent. The modern mind finds it easier to imagine a universe held together by the equivalent of very tiny rubber bands than to talk about God, the devil, heaven, hell, or immortality. Yet the one unarguable fact that we do know about life is that each of us, and all of our loved ones, will die. Most of us sooner than we think. So the question, "Good Teacher, what must I do to inherit eternal life?" is the single most urgent and compelling question faced by every generation. *What must I do to be saved?* The answer to that question is the only information that finally matters. What happens *after* our deaths hinges on what we do here and now with our lives.

Every autumn we see in nature the signs of approaching winter. These signs remind us that death is part of life. Likewise, every fall, the Church calls us to the Solemnity of All Saints and the Feast of All Souls. These days belong to the Church calendar for a reason. They remind us of three important things: our own mortality; the destination God intends for each of us; and our need to pray for the dead.

Why do the dead need our prayers? It's very simple. All through life, we make choices. These choices make us what we become; in effect, we are the result of our choices. Even when we die in God's friendship, the consequences of some of our bad choices remain. They're like pieces of debris, which need to be purified or cleared away. Otherwise, they separate us from the fullness of God's joy. That purification is what we call purgatory. What exactly it consists of, we don't know, but the odds are good that most of us will make a stop there on our way home to God. Now, it's a very ancient Christian belief, rooted in Scripture and tradition, that we, the living, can speed the purification of those who have died in God's friendship by interceding for them with God through our prayers.

This is what we mean by the "communion of saints." The Church is a family, a communion. It's a communion not just horizontally, across cultures, but also vertically, through time. In fact, the old way of describing the Church as a family of three parts still has merit: the Church militant, we who live and preach Jesus Christ here on earth; the Church suffering, the souls in purgatory who have gone before us; and the Church triumphant, those souls who are now and forever with the Lord. The souls in heaven pray for us on earth. We on earth pray for those in purgatory. We help each other. We depend on each other. If God has a signature behavior, this is it: the mutual interdependence that flows from love, in this life and the next.

The Church often speaks of the "Four Last Things": death, judgment, hell, and heaven. She has a good reason for doing so. Whether we ever figure out the subatomic structure of the universe, we all will very soon encounter the Four Last Things, up close and personal. They are very real, and they matter eternally. When the young man asked Jesus, "Good Teacher, what must I do to inherit eternal life?" he was reminding us that each human soul has something to be saved for ... and something to be saved from. We are made for joy. We are made for heaven. But we have alternatives. St. Paul is sometimes criticized for being so urgent and even harsh in his tone. Yet Jesus, for all His tenderness, talks about damnation far more frequently than Paul does. Reread the parable of the talents in Matthew 25. Look at what happens to the weeds and the bad fish in the parables of Matthew 13.

We modern Christians tend to make Jesus effete in our popular piety, as an unconscious way of taming Him. Yet He didn't come to make us comfortable. C.S. Lewis once wrote that "the sweetly attractive human Jesus is a product of nineteenth-century skepticism, produced by people who were ceasing to believe in His divinity, but wanted to keep as much Christianity as they could."

Lewis warned that anyone coming to Scripture for the first time with an open mind might get something of a shock. He noted that "we [as creatures] are simply not *invited* to speak, to pass *any* moral judgment on [Jesus], however favorable; it is only too clear that *He* is going to do whatever judging there is; [and] it is *we* who are *being* judged, sometimes tenderly, sometimes with stunning severity." Jesus always makes clear the urgency and gravity of the gospel. There's a very good reason for that. Jesus understands what's at stake. He also knows the cost, in blood, of our redemption.

What does any of this have to do with growing in Christ? Everything. In our country, in our time, most of us live in an environment saturated with science, technology, and the rationalist approach to life that governs both. Each year we get more and more disconnected from nature and its sacramental message. Remember that nature itself is a kind of sacrament, a sign that points to God. When we reread the parables of Jesus, we immediately notice that so many of them are *organic*. They're about growth and abundance, because life is organic. Life is not an equation or a machine. Think about the mustard seed that grows into a mighty tree; the sower who plants and harvests; the loaves and the fishes; the vine and the branches. Even the parable of the talents is about stewards who do—or don't—grow their treasure into more than what they were given.

My point is not that ninety-two cable channels are useless, or that "string theory" is unimportant. Science and technology have brought us many good things. Yet, in a sense, we've allowed ourselves to become more foolish, not smarter, because of them. We're losing the vocabulary needed to seek and understand the really important information in life. Jesus did not say, "I am the way, the facts, and the database." He said, "I am the way, and the truth, and the life." There's a difference. Truth and life include scientific fact, but they're infinitely richer than that. One of the greatest scientists of all time—a man who dedicated his whole life to the dignity of human reason—was Blaise Pascal. He was also a faithful Catholic who lived in the center of the French Enlightenment. He wrote: "The heart has its reasons, which reason cannot know."

Reason is a gift of God, and a vital way of knowing both God and the world. Yet, when it becomes the *only* way of knowing, it ends by attacking, rather than ennobling, the human person. Eugenics, in its own way, is very "reasonable." It's also inhuman. It's easy to look back on Nazi eugenics experiments and condemn them as crimes against humanity, but eugenics is alive and well, right now and right here, in our own country. It wears better suits. It uses kinder words and has better public relations agents. Yet the message is the same: "Let's clean up the gene pool by getting rid of the garbage." Ask yourself why children with Down's syndrome are becoming extinct. It isn't because we're solving their problems. It's because we're "solving" *our* problem by killing them before they're born.

"Good Teacher, what must I do to inherit eternal life?" Here's the first step: Breathe with both your lungs. Use your mind and your heart. Seek the truth with your brain *and* your heart and your soul. Faith in Jesus Christ is more than just an item on your weekly "to do" list. It's more than just a piece in the puzzle of your life. *It's the heart of the matter.*

Go back to the parables of Jesus. Becoming a Christian

involves more than getting baptized. Living in Christ demands more than a born-again experience and going to church. Baptism is a mandate for action. Living in Christ requires daily conversion, discipleship, and transformation. Becoming a Christian and living in Christ imply *a lifetime of growing in Christ.* The water of Baptism gives life to the seed in our hearts that is Jesus Christ. The more the seed grows—the more we nourish and cultivate it through the sacraments, prayer, and apostolic action—the more we grow *into* Christ. We were made to do that. We were made to grow and bear the fruit of cooperating with Jesus in redeeming and sanctifying the world.

Of course, what doesn't grow dies. In Scripture, the tree that bears no fruit is cut down. Growing in Christ requires that we "change our heads," that we renew and enrich our way of knowing things. It asks that we begin to experience, understand, act in, and speak to the world in an entirely new way. How do we do that?

Back in 1988, Pope John Paul II published a document called *Christifideles Laici.* The full title in English is unfortunately rather daunting: *The Vocation and Mission of the Lay Faithful in the Church and in the World.* Yet, if you haven't read it, put it on your list. While it may sound demanding, it's actually very readable, and filled with wonderful counsel. Here's a little bit from it:

> The vocation of the lay faithful to holiness implies that life according to the Spirit expresses itself in a particular way in their involvement in temporal affairs and in their participation in earthly activities. Once again the apostle [Paul]

admonishes us: "Whatever you do, in word or deed, do everything in the name of the Lord Jesus, giving thanks to God the Father through him" [Col 3:17] (17).

John Paul continues in this way:

Therefore, to respond to their vocation, the lay faithful must see their daily activities as an occasion to join themselves to God, fulfill His will, serve other people and lead them to communion with God in Christ. (17)

He further states (emphasis added):

To be able to discover the actual will of the Lord in our lives always involves the following: *a receptive listening to the Word of God and the Church; fervent and constant prayer; recourse to a wise and loving spiritual guide; and a faithful discernment of the gifts and talents given by God,* as well as the diverse social and historic situations in which one lives.... [Moreover, it] is not a question of simply knowing what God wants from each of us in the various situations of life. The individual *must do what God wants,* as we are reminded in the words of Mary, mother of Jesus, addressed to the servants at Cana: "Do whatever He tells you" (Jn 2:5). However, to act in fidelity to God's will requires a capability for acting—and the development of that capability (58).

Growing in Christ is exactly how we develop that capability to know and carry out God's will. The Catholic faith is always personal, but never private. What that means is that each one of us is uniquely loved by God. As we've seen, the love story between God and each individual soul is unique, intensely personal, forever, and unrepeatable. God will never love another person in the same way He loves you. Yet, that's never the whole story of faith. In the wider community of believers, just as in any other family, real love always bears fruit in new life. Our faith in God—our love for Jesus Christ—must always bear fruit in bringing someone else to a new or deepened faith. Faith always has a communal dimension, what we call an *ecclesial* dimension. *Ekklesia* is the New Testament Greek word meaning "gathering" or church. Nobody can live his or her faith in a purely vertical way. Nobody owns a private telephone line to God. We all share the conversation, and a very important part of the conversation we have with God depends on the conversation we have with each other.

This is the heart of Catholic social doctrine. It's the first step to growing in Christ. True Christian belief is rarely an "either/or" experience, but rather a "both/and" experience. Catholic faith is *both* personal and communal, *both* individual and ecclesial. And for that matter, it's both scriptural and sacramental. Scripture and sacrament cannot be separated—a truth that unfortunately separates some of our Christian brothers and sisters from a full experience of Jesus Christ and His gospel.

Keeping this in mind, and building on the Holy Father's thoughts, here are five steps we can take to cooperate with God's grace and to grow in Christ. The first three are personal and individual. The last two are communal and ecclesial.

First, each of us needs to pray. We need to become persons

of prayer. In fact, according to St. Paul, we need to pray not just daily, but without ceasing. Of course, that sounds impossible, but with a little persistence, anybody can do it. Many of us have a secret and mistaken image of prayer left over from when we were young. We assume that praying is like an automobile assembly line. If we produce enough Hail Marys, we make our quota, and God will probably give us what we want. Or at least He won't be angry with us.

I certainly don't want to diminish the value of repetitive or formulaic prayer. Sometimes it's the only kind of prayer we can pray. Yet God isn't interested in production quotas. Remember the old Baltimore Catechism? It defined prayer as "the lifting up of a person's mind and heart to God." The great Eastern Father of the Church, St. John Damascene, described it as "the raising of one's mind and heart to God, or the requesting of good things from God." Yet my favorite definition of prayer comes from the Little Flower. St. Thérèse of Lisieux was regarded as dull-witted by some of her sisters in religious life. Today, she's a doctor of the Church and copatroness of the Church's universal missionary activity. Listen to her words: "For me, prayer is a surge of the heart; it is a simple look turned toward heaven; it is a cry of recognition and of love, embracing both trial and joy." In her autobiography, *The Story of a Soul*, she writes: "It's a terrible thing to admit, but saying the rosary takes it out of me more than any hair shirt would; I do say it so badly! Try as I will to put force on myself, I can't meditate on the mysteries of the rosary; I just can't fix my mind on them."

Finally, Thérèse concludes, "apart from [the Divine Office], I can't face the strain of hunting about in books for these splendid prayers—they make my head spin. There are such a lot of them, each more splendid than the last; how am I to recite them all, or to choose between them? I just do what children have to do before they've learned to read: I tell God what I want quite simply, without any splendid turns of phrase, and somehow He always manages to understand me."

John the Evangelist tells us that "God is love." God Himself tells us in Scripture that He wants not our burnt offerings and holocausts, but our love. The form of our personal prayers is much less important than the heart behind it. Those of you who are married know that the usual expressions of love within a marriage—flowers, gifts, the words "I love you"—are important and beautiful. Yet, what moves the heart like an earthquake is when a spouse does something unexpected—out of love—that is unique, unselfish, spontaneous, and sincere.

So, too, with God. He wants our love. He wants our attention. The sincere gift of our self is important. How we do it—the wrapping on the gift—is secondary. We might even take it a step further. When we focus too much on the technique of prayer, we can subtly reduce God to an instrument of our wants, and shift the focus to our own efforts. The only "technique" Jesus told us to use is the Our Father. Beyond that, any form of prayer, from the most ancient and venerated to the most spontaneous and personal, will do the trick. The point is to try. The point is to persist, whenever and wherever we can turn our hearts to God.

Here's another point about prayer. Though we pray for four basic reasons, the first three get the lion's share of our attention: (1) We ask God for things we want and need, including His forgiveness; (2) We praise Him for His greatness; (3) We thank Him for His gifts. Yet we often overlook another very important kind of prayer: We should pray in order *to listen for God's will.* Remember the words of Mary to the servants at Cana: "Do whatever He tells you." We can't hear what God wants to tell us if we don't cultivate a habit of listening, along with the inner silence it requires. Prayer is not a monologue. God knows us better than we know ourselves. If we listen, sooner or later we'll feel His presence.

In his essay "Work and Prayer," C.S. Lewis quoted an old Latin saying, *laborare est orare*—"to work is to pray." Work can never take the place of prayer, but it can certainly be a fruitful form of prayer. We can "pray without ceasing" because everything we do and experience can be lifted up as a prayer to our Father. That includes our work, joys, achievements, and disappointments, and most especially our sufferings. John Paul II wrote in *On the Christian Meaning of Suffering* that each person, in his or her personal suffering, becomes "a sharer in the redemptive suffering of Christ" (19). He added that "every human suffering, by reason of [a person's] loving union with Christ, completes the suffering of Christ. It completes that suffering *just as the Church completes the redemptive work of Christ*" (24).

This is why the Church reveres the "creative" character of suffering—because "in suffering there is concealed a particular power which draws the person interiorly close to Christ" (26). Even the worst suffering, when given over to God, has power and meaning as prayer. Scripture is filled with examples, which is why the Holy Father describes the Bible as "a great book about suffering" (6).

This leads to a second practical step we can take toward growing in Christ. We need to read the Scriptures—not just read them, but immerse ourselves in them, always relying on the guidance and encouragement of the Church. The Word of God is a vital way in which Jesus continues His presence among us. In fact, the great Western Father of the Church, St. Jerome, once wrote that "Ignorance of the Scriptures is ignorance of Christ." Vatican II, in its *Dogmatic Constitution on Divine Revelation,* urged all Christians to read and pray over Sacred Scripture frequently, because "the nourishment [offered by Scripture] enlightens the mind, strengthens the will and fires the hearts of men with the love of God" (23).

The third practical step we can take toward growing in Christ is like the second, but broader. We need to read *about* the faith, and not just in Sacred Scripture. We need to renew our acquaintance with all kinds of good Christian literature, from the ancient Fathers, like John Chrysostom, to the novelists of this century. The *Confessions* by Augustine still stands as the best conversion story in history, fifteen hundred years after he wrote it. If you read *The Great Divorce* or *The Screwtape Letters,* by C.S. Lewis, or his essays in *The Problem of Pain,* you'll never again doubt the likelihood of hell. If you want a glimpse of purgatory, read Tolkien's short story, "Leaf by Niggle". *The End of the Affair* and *The Power and the Glory* are wonderful novels of faith by Graham Greene. For a taste of heaven, read *The Last Battle* in C.S. Lewis' *The Chronicles of Narnia.*

Of course, there's so much more. Authors like Flannery O'Connor, Walker Percy, Chesterton, Bernanos, Mauriac, and Guardini. Theologians like DeLubac and von Balthasar. The

wonderful—and very readable—documents of the Second
Vatican Council. The *Catechism of the Catholic Church*. And
don't forget the writings of Pope John Paul II, who has
renewed the entire outline of our Catholic faith over the past
twenty-plus years. Buy good Catholic literature. Read it. Share
it with other people. Reading directly helps us grow in Christ,
by educating, inspiring, encouraging, and motivating our
hearts. It gives us key information that is missing from the culture around us. It also creates interior silence, which allows God
to speak to us from the page.

A fourth step toward growing in Christ is deepening our
involvement in the larger mission of the Church. That begins
above all in the "domestic Church"—the family. Our families
need to come first, because that's where our Christian witness
can be most intimate and fruitful. Outside the home, the parish
is always the first place we should offer our time and skills.
Support the ministry of your pastor with your prayers, your presence, and your material help. For those who want to do more,
the vineyard is very big. Your financial support for the Church's
missionary work can make a huge difference. Helping financially
is a way for people who can't go on mission to share in the
Church's missionary mandate. Your parish and diocese are filled
with good ministries and evangelizing efforts which need your
presence. Get involved. Support and encourage each other. The
Epistle of James says that faith without works is a dead faith.
A *living* faith always bears fruit in action, both personal and
ecclesial. That's why we read the "Acts" of the Apostles, and not
the "Interesting Ideas," "Pious Sentiments," or "Good
Intentions" of the Apostles. Words are easy. Action counts.

Fifth and finally, we grow in Christ most fruitfully when we nourish ourselves on the sacraments. Too many married couples live their daily lives as if their wedding covenant was a beautiful ceremony in the past. In fact, the Sacrament of Matrimony is an *ongoing* source of strength for husbands and wives. Christ is permanently present in the marriage covenant, the "third partner" in every marriage, and eager to comfort and encourage married couples who turn to Him. So it is also with priests and deacons, whom Christ uniquely configures to Himself in the Sacrament of Holy Orders. The Sacrament of Holy Orders happens only once. Yet its imprint is forever, and it offers a constant source of renewal for those men who understand that being configured to the cross of Christ also means being configured to His fruitfulness and His resurrection. Finally, the Sacrament of the Anointing of the Sick not only prepares us for death, but can also offer us a source of Christ's spiritual and even physical healing in any serious illness.

Here, we've focused especially on the Sacraments of Initiation—Baptism, Confirmation, and the Eucharist—and we've done that for a reason. These are the channels of God's grace that create, confirm, and sustain our new life in Jesus Christ.

Yet "new life in Christ" makes no sense outside an awareness of our own sinfulness, our need for redemption, repentance, conversion, and reconciliation with God. The key to unlocking the richness of the Eucharist and the fullness of the Christian life is the Sacrament of Penance, which prepares the heart to recognize and receive its Savior. The more fully we understand this sacrament, the more vividly we grasp the gift of the Eucharist.

The most important single thing any of us can do to grow in Christ, reform our hearts, renew the Church, and change the world is simply this: *Go back to Confession, regularly and sincerely.* Forgive and seek forgiveness. Everything else will follow.

John Paul II writes, near the end of *Christifideles Laici*, that "There cannot be two parallel lives in [our] existence: on the one hand, the so-called 'spiritual' life with its values and demands; and on the other, the so-called 'secular' life, that is, life in a family, at work, in social relationships, in the responsibilities of public life and in culture.... This split between the faith which many [of us] profess and [our] daily lives deserves to be counted among the more serious errors of our age" (59).

"Good Teacher, what must I do to inherit eternal life?" This is the only question that finally matters, especially in an "age of missing information." Jesus answers it: "Come, follow Me."

Growing in Christ is the road we walk in His footsteps.

CHAPTER FOUR

Eucharist

In its *Constitution on the Sacred Liturgy* (SC), Vatican II described the Eucharist as the source and summit of Catholic life (10). Let's take a closer look at why.

Pope John Paul II has said that the liturgical renewal promoted by the Second Vatican Council should be "the prime agent of the wider renewal of Catholic life." He has also stressed that the root of any new evangelization must be a personal encounter with Jesus Christ. Where do we most intimately encounter Christ? We find Him in the Scriptures and prayer, of course, but John Paul II also points to the unique presence of Jesus in the Liturgy, and especially to His real presence in the Blessed Sacrament (*Church in America*, 12).

Encountering Jesus by making the Eucharist the center of our lives may be a bigger challenge than we suspect. Many Catholics, sometimes even among the clergy, tend to take the Eucharist for granted. Yet, only through a deeper understanding of—and reverence for—the Eucharist can we enter into the joy of the Lord which the Great Jubilee celebrated. Moreover, leading others to this great encounter with the Lord is at the heart of our mission as believers.

Vatican II wanted to make Christians enthusiastic again about living their faith and bringing it to the whole world. That's why the Council Fathers reformed the Liturgy in the first place. They understood that the goal of all apostolic work is to bring women and men together in the Church to praise God: "to take part in the Sacrifice and to eat the Lord's Supper" (SG10). They also taught that, through the Liturgy, God's grace poured out on us "as from a fountain," so that all Church activity could be accomplished with great fruitfulness. Yet, for the Liturgy to be fully effective, the faithful needed to worship with the right heart. Herein lay the greatest pastoral challenge and the reason for all the conciliar reforms of external practice: *to help the faithful lift up their hearts.* Often in Church history, we've been guilty of overemphasizing liturgical externals, but the duty of all those who have pastoral responsibility regarding the Liturgy was spelled out by the Council Fathers: "to ensure that the faithful take part [in the Liturgy] *fully aware* of what they are doing, actively engaged in the rite and enriched by it" (11).

Awareness, engagement, and enrichment are matters of the heart. Dealing with the human heart is a sensitive and great responsibility. So often sorrow, doubt, or anxiety weighs down the soul. This is why, at the preface of the Eucharistic Canon, the celebrant calls the assembly to "lift up your hearts." When the assembly responds, "We lift them up to the Lord," the People of God remind themselves that in the face of the darkness that sometimes surrounds them, Christ has won the victory of good over evil. This involves a great act of faith and love. Mere sentiment cannot meet the heart's needs. A person's deepest longings can only be met by *possessing the truth in love.*

The Desert Fathers said that the battle for the heart is waged in the mind. This reminds us of our need to provide our people with much better teaching about the Liturgy.

The Second Vatican Council called for a full, conscious, and active participation by all Catholics in the Liturgy. What does it mean to "participate" in the Liturgy—not just for priests, deacons, and other ministers, but also for the whole assembly? Today, too many Catholics assume that taking part in the Liturgy almost requires us to be involved in a liturgical ministry of one kind or another. Some presume that if we're not involved in a formal ministry, we're more of a spectator than a participant. Others feel frustrated because they see in the norms guiding participation a lack of spontaneity, and along with it, a lack of authenticity. Some even change or ignore uncomfortable parts of a ritual in a misguided attempt to "improve" participation.

We need to remember that the Liturgy is the Church at prayer: a perfect prayer offered through Christ to the Father in the power of the Holy Spirit. But why should we join in the worship? Do we do it for God or for ourselves, the People of God? The answer depends on our perspective.

From God's side, the Eucharistic Liturgy is a moment of communion and mission with and for His people. The Liturgy becomes a place where He can give Himself—Father, Son, and Holy Spirit—to His people so that they can possess and enjoy Him. In this possession and enjoyment, He empowers them and then sends them out to bring His love to the world until the end of time. From the human point of view, the Liturgy is worship that we offer God. This may seem presumptuous. God doesn't need us to tell Him that He's God. Nonetheless, we believe that limited and selfish creatures like ourselves are empowered to offer God something of eternal value. We can do so because we participate in Christ's work of redemption, which not only saves us from sin but also raises us to divine life. Through the Liturgy, we become godly instruments of praise: revealing, magnifying, and extending God's glory and the greatness of His love.

Therefore, the purpose of Mass is the praise of God and the sanctification of the human person. Again, God doesn't "need" our praise, but as Augustine teaches in the *Confessions,* He created us so that we would find our happiness in praising Him. This praise is an intimately *personal* work for each one of us, but, as we saw earlier, it is not *private.* A crucial difference exists here. "Personal" and "private" do not mean the same thing. Catholics are not rugged individualists when it comes to faith. We worship together, in relationship to others, through the Church. This means we're called to participate in the Liturgy *together,* genuinely united in our hearts and minds.

Similarly, our sanctification is not a "private" thing. God sanctifies us together, in the Church, so that all our relationships become holy. What's the nature of this holiness? For Christians, holiness consists of charity—the friendship and love of God. That same love which is exchanged among the Father, Son, and Holy Spirit is given to us, to make us holy. The more God sanctifies us, the more we feel the simultaneous need to be in union with Him, and in right relationship with all those He has created along with us. To participate fully in the Mass means to submit our whole human experience to God, worshiping together with the people of God, in a way that takes up our full intelligence, our full freedom, and our whole heart.

The entire assembly is called to take part in the Eucharist. To ensure this participation, the Holy Spirit created different ministries in the Church. These ministries all serve the royal priesthood which all of us—lay, religious, and ordained—share. Each of us receives the royal priesthood at Baptism, and we each have it strengthened at Confirmation. Through this royal priesthood, the baptized are joined to the prayers of Jesus in the heavenly Liturgy, so that their prayers are united to His before the Father. Through the prayer and adoration offered by the royal priesthood, the Church cooperates in Christ's work of redemption and brings it to bear on the real-life situations of God's people today. Accordingly, in 1 Peter we read that "you are a chosen race, a royal priesthood, a holy nation, God's own people, that you may declare the wonderful deeds of him who called you out of darkness into his marvelous light" (2:9).

The royal priesthood is served in a uniquely important way by the *ministerial* priesthood, the priesthood bestowed on those who receive the Sacrament of Orders as priests and bishops. The roles of the royal priesthood and the ministerial priesthood are fully equal in dignity, but *complementary in nature*—in other words, they're distinct by God's design, and never purely functional or interchangeable. The better we understand this truth, the better it will help us to participate in the Liturgy.

The ordained priest, through the Sacrament of Holy Orders, is configured permanently to Christ. This empowers him to act in the person of "Christ the head," and this further enables him to lead the assembly, the body of Christ, into a sacred banquet,

a feast of sacrificial love. He does this not by an arbitrary impo-
sition of his own will but by following a plan revealed by the
Holy Spirit to the Church. This plan is called a ritual, and the
celebrant knows how to follow it, because of the norms and
rubrics it contains. Local bishops can, of course, culturally adapt
this plan, but they must also ensure that the plan's integrity is
never compromised. The *purpose* of the ritual is to protect the
unity of worship of the whole Church, through every culture,
in every part of the world. Ritual leads the celebrant, other ministers, and the assembly to freely perform their complementary
roles. As Catholics, we believe the rituals we celebrate in our
liturgies are the work of the Holy Spirit in the Church. This is
why we have confidence when lifting up our hearts in the manner called for by the Church. Sacred ritual helps humanity grow
accustomed to divine things—and it teaches each person how
to join his or her heart and mind with those of others.

Of course, our worship of God requires much more than just
following ritual. Full participation in the Liturgy means that the
whole assembly needs to take the joys, sorrows, and anxieties of
daily life and join them to the prayer of Jesus Christ before the
Father. Plenty of things get in the way. More often than not, the
obstacles to worship lie deep in our own hearts. Anything that
weighs down our hearts can prevent us from raising them up.
Only repentance, ongoing conversion, prayer, fellowship, and
catechesis can overcome the barriers to our participation in the
Liturgy. The secret to participating fruitfully in our worship has
less to do with external changes than it does with interior transformation. Again, a personal return to penance and reconciliation is the vital first step to recovering the riches offered to us in

the Eucharist. Ritual, rubrics, and pious practices take their proper place only when lived by a contrite people. People who have forgiving and forgiven hearts know that the struggle to lay down their lives for one another lies at the core of the Christian life—and they find in their rituals the freedom to worship in love.

Worshiping in love requires that we contemplate Jesus' presence when we celebrate the Eucharist. To contemplate Christ means to behold Him with the eyes of faith. This is especially important today, because so many of those who leave the Church do so because they've been discouraged and do not see Jesus Christ. The disciples on the road to Emmaus knew the same discouragement. When Jesus came to them, they didn't recognize Him. He questioned them about their discouragement, and instead of recognizing Him, they spoke of defeat and death. So, very gently, He admonished them, explaining to them the Scriptures. Still, they didn't recognize Him—but they did invite Him to share a meal. With that invitation, He transformed their table into a Eucharist, and they recognized Him in the breaking of the bread. From this recognition—this contemplation of Christ and intimately personal experience of His love—they immediately went forth to proclaim the Good News. In like manner, Catholics can be delivered from the discouragement that prevents us from proclaiming the Good News only if we can really see Jesus Christ in the Liturgy.

The reason for this is simple. Beholding Christ leads us to take part in His great mystery of sacrificial love. In the Mass, Jesus is present as our head in the person of the priest, gathering us together and uniting our hearts and our gifts with His.

Christ's body is present in the entire assembly gathered in prayer, revealing the unity of love Christ has with the Father through the assembly's unity in words and actions. Jesus the eternal Word is present when the Scriptures are proclaimed and the demands of the covenant are preached. Yet, in a real, special, and very powerful manner, He is also present in the Eucharist as the perfect sacrifice, the medicine of immortality, and the antidote for death.

After the priest says the words of institution, our gifts of bread and wine truly become Jesus' Body and Blood, soul and divinity. In the Eucharistic Prayer, Jesus Christ present on the altar offers Himself to our Father in heaven, so that the work of redemption accomplished at Calvary will bear fruit in our lives today. Through the sacrifice of Jesus, our prayers and the prayers of the entire assembly are made fruitful, so that they have a real effect in the world we inhabit. At the same time, the Father truly delights in our praise. So, at Mass, heaven and earth literally touch. Our praise, because it's been purified and united to Christ, is pleasing to God, and it anticipates the praise and glory of heaven.

In the Eucharist, this gift of Christ's presence is given to us not only so we can offer Jesus to the Father. It's also provided to us as real food—spiritual nourishment that sustains us on our earthly pilgrimage. The Communion rite is an especially beautiful moment in the Eucharistic liturgy. The sacred character of this moment is revealed best by the prayer we offer together just before approaching the altar: *"Lord, I am not worthy to receive you, but only say the word, and I shall be healed."* This phrase echoes the words of the centurion who petitioned Christ for the healing of his servant. Jesus *marveled* at this extraordinary expression of faith, which allowed Him to reveal *"the immeasurable riches of His grace."*

The Church asks us to have exactly the same reverent faith whenever we receive our Lord's Body and Blood. Today the faithful come to Communion far more frequently than in the past, which is a very good thing. Yet I often wonder if we really understand the reverence and interior preparation for which receiving the Eucharist calls. Again, this is why a regular, personal devotion to the Sacrament of Penance always leads to a deeper experience of the Eucharist.

John Paul II has said that "In the Sacrament of the Eucharist the Savior, who took flesh in Mary's womb twenty centuries ago, continues to offer Himself to humanity as the source of divine life." Our mission today is the same as it has always been: to bring Jesus Christ to those who need Him most. This mission includes building a whole civilization of love—which has, at its center, a culture of life and a respect for human dignity and rights. Part of that task is to engage our secular contemporaries in a morally compelling way. In the United States, the rugged individualism embedded in our pioneer spirit needs to be reexamined. We should also recognize that many people in our society are already secretly weary of consumerism. They know that they won't—and can't—find the meaning of life in acquiring more things. It's useful here to remember the timeless words of Augustine, speaking about fifth-century Rome.

The only joy which they attained had the fragile brilliance of crystal, a joy far outweighed by the fear that it would be shattered in an instant.

Fear and isolation threaten the modern heart because, deep down, people are hungry for a more authentic experience of life. We yearn for the truth about our purpose in the world. We long for the deeper life that Jesus in the Eucharist makes possible. Yet, at the same time, the most serious challenge to our faith is subtler than anything in our culture. Rather, it's *our own* lack of zeal, *our own* discouragement and doubt. Why aren't we more vigorous in preaching and teaching the faith? It's because the task of taking up the cross of Christ can be arduous and embarrassing. We can evade the mission God gives us, and we often do. We can distract ourselves with toys, career, travel, and entertainment. In the process, though, we become spectators. We learn to watch life rather than live it.

Spectators don't contribute. They merely consume. Too often, in recent decades, we've carried this consumer attitude into the Liturgy. Instead of losing ourselves in worship of the Trinity and love for one another, we're preoccupied by what we *are* or *aren't* "getting out" of the Mass. We expect—and even train—musicians and other ministers to entertain us, rather than lead us in prayer. In the process, we've too often lost our sense of awe, our reverence for Jesus in the Eucharist, and our Christ-centered service to one another. In our spiritual sleep, vital moments of grace pass us by, while the young, lonely, and poor of our world suffer a new crucifixion, alone and without our support. The words of the great Eastern Father, John Chrysostom, speak to us very powerfully today, just as they did fifteen hundred years ago:

You have tasted the Blood of the Lord, yet you do not recognize your brother.... You dishonor this table when you do not judge worthy of sharing your food, someone judged worthy to take part in this meal.... God freed you from all your sins and invited you here, but you have not become merciful.

The Eucharist is infinitely more than just a symbol, or memory, or pious ritual. Christ in this sacrament is real and present. The *living, tangible, flesh-and-blood presence* of Jesus in the Eucharist commits us to the poor and wounded of our world. Their hunger and thirst must become our hunger and thirst. Only a whole civilization of love can provide for these kinds of needs. The engine by which such a civilization can be built is the Liturgy, which is the source and summit of God's love for us. Only the love that comes from God and goes to God is powerful enough to heal the wounds of our brothers and sisters, in this and every age. If we truly believe in the real presence of Christ in the Eucharist, *and we act on it,* then others will clearly see and want the joy that is ours. If we enter more deeply into the solidarity of love that the Holy Spirit offers us in the Liturgy, then God will use us to sanctify the world.

As believers, our task in the Liturgy involves working to recover *the right focus and the proper reverence* in our worship. The Mass is not a show, or a performance, or a kind of entertainment. The Eucharist is about God. It should focus our worship and our hearts where they belong—on Him, not on us. We're important, because Jesus died for us, but we're secondary in the act of worship. Thus, our musicians, liturgists, acolytes, lectors, and extraordinary ministers of Holy Communion—all the wonderful people who serve in these roles—need to become transparent, humble, and deeply faithful to the Liturgy that the Church defines, so that nothing distracts us from our encounter with God.

An English Russian Orthodox bishop, Anthony Bloom, once used an image that we should take to heart. He said that the best surgeon's gloves are those that are so transparent and flexible that they're neither seen nor felt. If so, then the surgeon can work marvelous things through them. If the gloves are opaque, soiled, or rigid, they get in the way. They hinder the surgeon rather than help him. So, too, with our worship, our pastoral service, and our daily lives. The more unselfish we are, the greater the work Jesus will accomplish through us. In the Liturgy and in our lives of service, we need to become *less* so that Jesus will become *more*. We need to become invisible, so that God will become ever more visible.

CHAPTER FIVE

"Light to the Nations"

The crisis of our day is a crisis of unbelief. Luke's Gospel says: "When the Son of Man comes, will he find any faith on earth?" (Lk 18:8). It's an unsettling question. When Catholics look at our grandchildren and children, and we reflect on the political climate of our time on issues like abortion, euthanasia, and care for the homeless and the poor, that same question rises in our hearts. Will the Son of Man find any faith when He comes again?

Pope John XXIII opened the windows of the Church to the modern world. Because of him, the Church at Vatican II rightly sought to baptize what is best in the societies around us and renew herself by learning from the many good things found in secular and non-Christian cultures. Unfortunately, John Paul II has had the much more difficult task of encouraging the world to open its windows to the Church. So, as we look back over the decades since the Second Vatican Council, we notice that our dialogue with the world has been largely one-sided. The secular world hasn't been particularly interested in what the Church has to say.

Here's the point: The Church makes her greatest public

contribution when she remains true to her own message and mission. The Church best serves the world not by trying to "accommodate" the world, but by being faithful to the mandate of Jesus Christ. The more faithful we remain to the gospel, the more useful we are to the world. When the Church seems to be "against" the world, she is against the world *for the sake of the world*—so that the world might come to know its Savior and the truth that makes it free.

A "culture war" is taking place throughout our society—in education, in the arts, in law, in politics, in the entertainment media, even within the Church. At the heart of this conflict are competing moral visions of what human beings are meant to be, and how we define ourselves as a country. On one side, many people emphasize individual liberty, the ideal of personal choice, and the notion of self-fulfillment—in other words, the way to happiness is to fulfill ourselves. On the other side, many people stress that we're communal beings by nature and that we have responsibilities for the common good. These people also talk about freedom—but a different kind of freedom. Not so much the freedom to choose, but the freedom to do what is right and good.

One group emphasizes autonomy, arguing that human dignity consists of being unfettered and independent. In other words, we create ourselves, and joy and happiness are found in this self-creation. The other group emphasizes that we are created by Someone who is greater than we are. We are creatures. We are not autonomous. We are made in the image of God, and we must be faithful to the moral order God has given us. We don't invent the moral order. We discover it, and then we struggle to become faithful to it.

Radically different views of the world inform these distinct moral visions. They bear some discussion. To be Catholic, we don't have to believe that the Church has something to say about everything in life, or that she has detailed plans for political activity and economic organization. In fact, she doesn't. The world has its proper autonomy from religion. Jesus Himself said so when He told us to render to Caesar the things which are Caesar's. So we don't need to live in a theocracy where religion is the dominant political force. Nor is the Church usually in the business of telling us for whom to vote, or of trying to come up with a social system that works. The Church recognizes that a legitimate, autonomous space exists for the "secularity" of the world and for the order of worldly affairs outside herself, like politics.

Secularity and "secularism" are two very distinct animals, however. Secularism is the refusal to admit that God has anything to say about the world. This perspective suggests that we may practice our faith on Sundays, but we live in quite a different world Monday through Saturday. Politicians who say they personally oppose abortion, but then don't work to change the laws in order to protect unborn life, are examples of the most damaging kind of secularism. Their faith life has virtually no effect on their public service. Secularism implies that the world no longer needs God. It can involve direct unbelief, which is true atheism, or the atheism of indifference, in which God doesn't have any practical effect. Secularism participates in the sin of Adam and Eve, who wanted to be like God. We substitute ourselves for our Creator.

If the Church herself is divided on some of today's most sensitive issues, the divisions are usually rooted in differences about her self-understanding. A key question for all of is: What should Catholics believe about the Church? What role does the Church play in our understanding of the Christian life?

To answer that, we need to reflect on the single most important document from the Second Vatican Council. It's called *Lumen Gentium,* or the *Dogmatic Constitution on the Church.*

Lumen Gentium is a Latin title. The words mean "light to the nations." The Church should be the light of Christ to the world around us. All other documents of Vatican II deal with some aspect of the Church. Each one of those is a product of the Holy Spirit operating in the life of the Church, so we should never minimize their importance. Yet what is so foundational about *Lumen Gentium* is that it talks about the *whole* Church, her entire mission and identity.

Lumen Gentium describes the Church in a number of important ways. It speaks of the Church as being the sacrament of Christ. We should be able to look on the Church and see Jesus Christ, who is not visibly present to us in other ways. Just as the Church is a sacrament of Christ, Christ is a sacrament of God. We look on the face of Jesus, and we see what God is like. In Jesus' forgiveness, we see God's forgiveness. In Jesus' love, we see God's love for us. Thus, just as the seven sacraments are individual signs of Christ's presence in the Church, and the Church herself is a symbol of Christ's presence in the world, so, too, Jesus was and is a sacrament of His Father. Jesus is also the "sacrament of humanity." When we look on the face of Jesus, we see not only what God is like, but also what we are supposed to be like. Jesus is the perfect child of God. In His life and in His love, in the way He related to God and in the way He related to His sisters and brothers, we find our deepest meaning as human beings.

We who belong to the Church are commissioned to be Jesus' presence in the world. Because of that, the Church must continually carry out the threefold ministry of Jesus. He preached the Good News; He built up the community of believers; and He served those around Him, especially those most in need. That's what the Church should be today. Catholics are meant to be a reflection of Christ's presence in the world, preaching the gospel, spreading the kingdom of God, building up the community of the faithful, and then reaching out to those who are most in need. If we don't do all of these things, we're not the full, clear presence of Christ in the world.

This is the Church's self-understanding. Yet the Church also says many other things about herself. For example, the Church claims that Jesus Christ founded her, and that might seem obvious, but many people today don't really believe it. Some theologians very explicitly don't believe it. Alfred Loisy, a French theologian in the late nineteenth century, was one of the founders of Modernism, a heresy that tried to update the faith by "demythologizing" it. One of the things he said has many echoes in our own time: "Jesus preached the kingdom of God ... and the Church came instead." We may laugh at that, but where Loisy once stood, other people stand today. They don't identify the Church with Jesus. They don't see Jesus as the founder of the Church as we know her. They perceive the Church much more as an organization created by the apostles and those who followed them, to help accomplish their mission. Yet the Catholic faith holds—and has always held—that Jesus Christ founded the Church, as we know her. Therefore, she is a gift from Jesus to all of us. She is not something we can reorganize or dispose of as we wish.

Lumen Gentium also speaks of the Church in biblical images. If we want to know the Church, we have to read the Bible. We're a people of the Living Word. The Bible came from God through the Church, but the Scriptures also stand in judgment on the Church. Therefore we need to be faithful to the Church's self-understanding as found in the Scriptures. Some of the biblical images are well worth recalling. Let's review just a few:

The Church as sheepfold. Often we don't feel comfortable with this metaphor, especially those of us who know sheep. They can be unpleasant animals and also rather mindless. They go where the grass is greener, and they don't care about too much else. Yet Jesus Himself uses this image. The reason He uses it, of course, is because of the importance of the shepherd, the Good Shepherd. His sheep hear His voice and respond instinctively. They trust and they give themselves to the Shepherd.

The Church as temple and stones. The Church is the temple of God, and we are the living stones. Each one of us is infinitely important. The Church crumbles without our talents and gifts.

The Church as vine and branches. Jesus said, "I am the vine, and you are the branches" (Jn 15:5). That image speaks of our interconnectedness with one another and with God. If we're clipped from the vine and cut off from our source of nourishment, we wither and die. We are also one another's connection to Jesus. We're branches together.

The Church as spouse of Christ. The Church is the spouse of Jesus. Those readers who are married understand this more vividly and realistically than do those of us who aren't and who tend to romanticize marriage. Obviously, spouses aren't always happy with one another. Yet they're faithful—and in their struggles they share everything, if the marriage is going to work. Then peace and a kind of joy can grow, a joy that is indescribable, the joy of being loved by your spouse.

Of course, the two biblical images that especially stand out about the Church are the People of God and the Body of Christ. We are the Body of Christ. St. Paul tells us that. Christ is the Head, and we are the members. We need to see in this image the intermingling of the human and divine. The human and divine elements of the Church are not divisible. They're one interlocking reality. Christ is always a part of the Body, which is the Church. Scripture does not say that the Church is *like* the Body of Christ. It says the Church *is* the Body of Christ. Those are two very different notions, because "is" means it's a reality, while "like" means it's just a metaphor. We're told that *we are* the Body of Christ.

The metaphor from *Lumen Gentium* that truly captured the imagination of theologians during Vatican II was the Church as the People of God. This was a revolutionary concept for many of us. We had tended to think of the Church as the pope and the bishops, then the priests, and then the religious. Finally, the poor little laypeople sat at the bottom of the pyramid. Vatican II reconnected us with the beautiful, simple notion that the Church is God's people. All of us are the Church. Of course, that's quite distinct from saying, "I am the Church." We are the

Church together. When people are angry at their pastor, they will sometimes say to him, "well, don't forget, we're the Church," or "you told us, we're the Church!" And it's true. But that "we" isn't just you or me. It's us together. We are all the Church together, and any time part of her is missing, the Church is not whole.

Another key thing to notice in this image of the "People of God" is that the determining words are "of God," not "People." We come to our true identity by being the people who belong to God. We are God's possession. If we are not God's possession, we're just wandering nomads, lost in the desert, like the Jews before they came to the Promised Land. So it's very important for us to emphasize the whole concept—that we are the People of God who now constitute the Body of Christ.

Any time we emphasize one image of the Church at the expense of the others, we get into trouble. Heresy is rarely the denial of truth. Heresy is almost always the emphasis of one truth over others *at the expense* of the others. We emphasize the divinity of Christ over His humanity, or we stress the humanity of Christ over His divinity; or we praise the role of the laity over the hierarchy, or the role of the hierarchy over the laity. Yet Catholics have always striven to be faithful to the whole gospel, the whole message of Jesus. We can't read just one epistle, like James, for example, outside the context of the whole New Testament; likewise with any other book of the Bible. So, too, with our images of the Church.

Lumen Gentium reaffirms the hierarchical nature of the Church. "Hierarchical" means that the Church is a type of

community organized according to the different rights, respon-
sibilities, and levels of authority among her members.
Laypeople, priests, deacons, bishops, and religious all have equal
dignity in the Church. We all share in the same royal priesthood.
Yet we also have very different duties. The organization of the
Church naturally reflects this.

Some people don't like this idea. Some people wanted
Vatican II to change this, but it didn't. Some critics even claim
that Pope John Paul II has "betrayed" the Second Vatican
Council and wants to drag us back to the 1950s. In reality, he's
trying to lead us into the real content of the real documents of
the council—what the documents really say and not what some
interpreters would like them to say. The Second Vatican Council
clearly emphasized the hierarchical dimension of our Church, *as
well as* the image of the Church as the People of God. If we're
going to be faithful to Vatican II, we need to be faithful to the
whole teaching.

A healthy family is not a dictatorship, but neither is it a
democracy. So, too, with the Church. Catholics give a unique
role to the pope and the bishops, who succeed the apostles of
the early Church. We do this not because we choose to, but
because we acknowledge that Jesus Christ has rightfully established their role. Therefore, Catholics believe not just in the
"primacy" of the pope, but *in his authority*. Catholics further
believe that the pope is infallible when he speaks *ex cathedra* on
matters of faith and morals.

We believe that no local Church—a local Church is a diocese—
is complete without an apostle. That's why the bishop is such a
vital part of each diocese. When I go out to do confirmations and

ask people what a bishop is, young people often have no idea. They think a bishop is someone who organizes and runs the Church. I say, "Well, why do we do it that way? The Baptists don't have bishops, and they seem to get along just fine." They reply, "Well, our way works better." We have this way of doing things, and it works better. Many young people view the role of the bishops as keeping people communicating and things smoothly organized, so that everybody will be happy. Yet the truth is that Catholics don't believe a local Church is complete without an apostle, and the bishops are successors to that role in our ecclesial communities. That's why we have dioceses.

Let's take it a step further. If I asked you what church you belong to, you'd probably say, "St. Mary's Parish," or "the Roman Catholic Church," or something similar. That's not the correct answer, however. Or rather, it's only partly correct. We do belong to the universal church, and we do belong to a particular parish, but the church we really belong to is our local church, our diocese. This isn't because the bishop may happen to be tall and dignified. I'm short and not always the most dignified person in the room. Rather, we believe that our bishops are direct successors to the apostles, and that this plays a critical role in our ecclesial realities, our dioceses, our churches.

We need to put this in the context of everything else in *Lumen Gentium* or we can easily skew our picture of the Church. We don't want to paint a portrait of the Church where somehow just the pope and the bishops are in charge, and nobody else counts. That's foolish. Everyday life is lived in our homes, not with the pope and the bishops. Yet the pope and the bishops do have a significant role, and it's a vital element of the

Catholic faith. Through them, the Church is promised guidance from Jesus until the end of time, in matters of faith and morals. This is not necessarily because of the wisdom or the goodness of her pastors, but because of the goodness and the wisdom of Jesus, who has given us His promise.

Lumen Gentium has a separate chapter on laypeople, and it undergirds much of what Pope John Paul II says about laypersons in *The Vocation and Mission of the Lay Faithful.* The unique role of laypeople is to sanctify the world. This doesn't mean that the "life of the outside world" is the only place where laypeople should function. Nor is it a way of keeping the laity out of the internal business of the Church. Rather, the gospel is most urgently needed in the building up of the faith in our families, at work, and in our neighborhoods, and in the transformation of society. That's where the action really lies, and that's the pre-eminent realm of laypeople.

One of the strangest tendencies today among some laypeople and even clergy is to assume that the real action is inside the Church. In other words, a person isn't really a Catholic unless he or she belongs to the parish council, or serves as an extraordinary minister of Holy Communion, or teaches religious education. This is simply wrong. What *Lumen Gentium* teaches is that we shouldn't serve the Church at the expense of the world. It's important for laypeople to be involved in the life of the Church as well, of course. Parish council and liturgy committee members are absolutely essential. *Yet, remember the world.* We're here for the world, to transform the world and bring it to Christ.

We should never emphasize the internal life of the Church at the expense of our mission to the world. Frankly, that happens far too often today. At times, so much conflict occurs within the Church that we're not free to be the Body of Christ for others. We become preoccupied with our own conflicts and with ourselves. We've also seen a tendency to clericalize the laity. We begin to think that the bureaucracies in chanceries or on parish staffs are where the action really is. They're not. The "action" in the Catholic faith is in our homes and in the marketplace.

Lumen Gentium also speaks about the "universal call to holiness." All of us are called to holiness. Bishops aren't called to any greater holiness than construction workers or janitors. We're all called to holiness through our Baptism, just as we're all personally called to be missionaries. We might have different responsibilities because of the particular roles we have in the Church, but we're all equally called to holiness.

Lumen Gentium finally reflects on the "eschatological" nature of the Church. That's an impressive word, but it simply means that this world isn't all there is. Much more exists than what we see around us. Something called heaven comes after this world, and in journeying there, we'll be judged on what we do now. When we talk about heaven, we don't diminish the world. In fact, we do just the opposite. We make what we do here more significant, because we're called to transform the earth.

Jesus Christ founded the Church for the salvation of the world. Yet in her present form she will one day disappear. The gates of hell will never prevail against her—Jesus promises that—but she won't forever be the sacramental presence of Christ. In the kingdom of God, we'll be with Jesus face to face.

We'll see the Father and the Holy Spirit face-to-face. During our sojourn on earth, however, the Church is here to remind us of God's eternal realities and to embrace us in Christ's already-present gift of eternal life. When this world ends—as it will someday—the Church will continue as the eternal bride of Christ in the wonderful marriage feast of heaven.

CHAPTER SIX

The Tug of Truth

One of the great feasts of the Church year is the Presentation of the Lord on February 2. Older Catholics may recall that the feast was once called the "Purification of the Blessed Virgin Mary," or Candlemas. One of the Scripture passages for the day comes from the Gospel of Luke. Mary and Joseph have brought the infant Jesus to the temple for the rites of purification:

> Now there was a man in Jerusalem, whose name was Simeon, this man was righteous and devout, looking for the consolation of Israel, and the Holy Spirit was upon him. And it had been revealed to him by the Holy Spirit that he should not see death before he had seen the Lord's Christ. And inspired by the Spirit he came into the temple; and when the parents brought in the child Jesus, to do for him according to the custom of the law, he took him up in his arms and blessed God and said, "Lord, now lettest thou thy servant depart in peace, according to thy word; for mine eyes have seen thy salvation which thou hast prepared in the presence of all peoples, a light for revelation to the Gentiles, and for glory to thy people Israel."

LUKE 2:25-32

"A light for revelation to the Gentiles." A light to the nations. That's the identity and mission of Jesus. That's the identity and mission of the Church He founded.

In living the basics of a Christian life, we soon discover the need to participate in a community of faith. By "community," of course, we mean the Church. The Church is our family of faith, the community of believers. To share in her life fruitfully, we need to understand two key conciliar documents: *Lumen Gentium*, which, as we've already seen, means "Light to the Nations," and *Gaudium et Spes*, which means "Joy and Hope." Jesus founded His Church to be a "light to the nations," and through her light—which is the light of the gospel—she becomes the source of humanity's "joy and hope."

In the last chapter, we focused on *Lumen Gentium*. While every document of Vatican II has value in understanding the Christian life, *Lumen Gentium* is the dogmatic constitution on the nature of the Church herself. Thus, in a sense, it ranks first among equals. *Gaudium et Spes*, the *Pastoral Constitution on the Church in the Modern World*, also has great importance. Yet it builds on and depends upon *Lumen Gentium*. As Catholics we can't be a source of joy and hope for anybody on the outside if we're dimming the light of the Church from the inside with bickering over who we are as a community.

One concern we should have today is that we've lost our awe for the Church. We hear frequently about the contrast between the "institutional Church" and the "real Church." We see this again and again in the newspapers. We read about what the "institutional Church" has to say or teach, and then we have it refuted by someone who claims to represent the "real Church," a spiritual entity separate from the institution. Yet this is not what Catholics believe. We have only one Church. Any distinction between an "institutional" Church and the "real" Church is both artificial and dangerous, because it gives us a license to choose what we want to believe and to throw away the rest. We set up a dishonest distinction between what the institutional Church teaches and what members of the "real" Church—in other words, we—prefer.

This kind of thinking relativizes the Church. Catholics once worried that their children might leave the Church for another faith. If children or grandchildren abandoned the Church, their salvation might be endangered. Today, many people feel that it doesn't really make much difference. The excuses are many: Those who leave are "following their consciences," they love God, they're trying to do what's good, and so on. Perhaps people say these things to console themselves or because they don't want to live with the tension of arguing with their children. Yet this attitude also frequently rises out of a lack of confidence that the Church *truly is* the Body of Christ and uniquely vital for our salvation.

If we claim to be Catholic, however, we must also profess that the Church *is* necessary. We can't relativize her mission away with soft words or sympathetic feelings. The Holy Father has stressed that the Church is "the universal sacrament of salvation," and "the sole means of salvation," and that the role of Christ and the Church in human salvation is absolutely unique.

Some people will refuse to accept this. Some may seek salvation outside the boundaries of the Church as we know her. Yet if a person really understands that the Church is the Body of

Christ, and that Christ's grace is available through the Church in a unique way, he or she is required to embrace the truth. That's the meaning of the doctrine, "There is no salvation outside the Church," which the Church has always taught, and still clearly teaches.

Catholics believe that the Catholic Church is the true Church. We believe other Christians are certainly loved by God. We believe that they do participate in the Church, even though they're separated from her fullness. Yet the Church has always taught, and always will teach, that *only the Catholic Church* has all those elements that Christ wishes His Church to have. Other churches do not. One or another Christian church may experience an aspect of the Christian life in a more vital way than we find in today's Catholic Church. Thus we need to acknowledge the gifts God gives to other faith communities, and learn from them. However, we're Catholics because we believe that *only the Catholic Church*—though she is sometimes inadequate or sinful in her members—is fully what God wants His Church to be.

Ask yourself this question: Why do we have a vocations crisis in the Church? Is it because of celibacy? I don't think so. When I was eighteen years old, my body wasn't any different from those of eighteen-year-old males today, and women were no less interesting, intelligent, and attractive in the 1960s than they are today. Yet somehow great numbers of young men were able to choose celibacy. Celibacy in the 2000s isn't the real obstacle to priestly vocations. Being faithful to celibacy has *always* involved a struggle. We have a crisis in priestly and religious vocations for the same reason we have a crisis in committed lay vocations: The sons and daughters of the Church lack confidence in the Church. No sensible person would become celibate for General Motors or Microsoft, and no sensible person should give himself as a celibate to the Church if the Church is merely an institution.

At the root of our vocations crisis is a lack of awe, love, and zeal for the Church. If we genuinely believe that the Church is the Body of Christ, then we'll enthusiastically give ourselves to her service—even if sacrifices are required—when we sense that God is calling us. *Our crisis of vocations results from the deeper crisis of faith in the Church.* Let's remember that when we stand up next Sunday after the homily and profess our faith. We say, "We believe in one holy, Catholic, and apostolic Church." Catholics believe in the Church. If we believe in the Church, then we must trust the Church when she speaks to us in the name of Jesus. We must not relativize her message, or diminish her authority.

This leads us to the issue of "orthodoxy." Orthodoxy is a Greek word, and a bad one in some contemporary circles. Orthodoxy means "correct teaching," or "right thinking." Is that narrow-minded? Is correct teaching insignificant? It's insignificant if we believe clear truth doesn't exist, or that truths are relative, or that very little truth can really be known. Yet, St. Paul said, "I am speaking the truth in Christ, I am not lying (Rom 9: 1).

When I was a young bishop, a teacher in an RCIA class at my cathedral parish told me, "There aren't very many things we need to believe to be a Catholic." That was news to me then, and it still is, today. We need to believe a great many things if we're Catholic. Minimizing them also minimizes the fact that we can know the truth, and the truth can make us free. Therefore, orthodoxy is not a "bad" word. On the contrary: orthodoxy is the Church's struggle to be faithful to her Lord. We need to be faithful with our minds as well as with our hearts, and we can't be faithful to, and we can't love, what we don't know. So the more we know about our faith, and the more faithful we are to the truths that Christ gives us, the more we can be faithful in our hearts to Jesus Christ.

After all, belief is what holds Catholics together as a community. Nothing else can bind us to one another if we don't share a commitment to Christ's truth. Not even love can do that. Love without truth is like faith without works—idealistic and ephemeral. So what we believe, and unity in what we believe, are vital to our life as a community. Correct belief was a crucial part of the early Church. "[There is] one Lord, one faith, one baptism," St. Paul told the Ephesians (Eph 4:5). The Athanasian Creed, more than fifteen hundred years old, says this: "Whoever will be saved, before all things, it is necessary that he hold the Catholic faith entire and unviolated."

Of course, a difference exists between being orthodox and being reactionary. So-called conservative people often don't serve the Church any better than so-called liberals. In fact, they can make the Church deeply unattractive. God is never served by vindictiveness. What serves the gospel—what serves the Church—is the longing to be faithful to the teachings of Jesus Christ.

These days, people sometimes can be very harsh toward theology and theologians. Yet, theology is important. There's a story told about an old man, who said, as he was dying, "I believe it all—true or false." That may sound pious, but it's not. Orthodoxy is about believing the truth. Theology helps us to know the truth. That's why Francis of Assisi told his brethren to respect theologians, and we should do the same. Of course, theologians should also have a profound reverence and respect for the Church. Theologians are not the Church's authoritative teachers. They do not have an authority that competes with the authority of bishops. Theologians are teachers, and they deserve our gratitude and respect, but theologians also need to be willing to be guided by the legitimate teaching authority of the Church—not controlled, but guided—if they hope to be faithful to their role in the Church.

Thus, orthodoxy is about truth and about the truth making us free. Since we know that Jesus is the way, the truth, and the life, we should long to be orthodox. Yet orthodoxy alone isn't enough. In Mark 6:30 we read: "The apostles returned to Jesus and reported to Him all that they had done and what they had taught." Note that the apostles not only told Jesus what they had taught. They also reported on what they had done—on their actions. Back in the 1970s and 1980s, liberation theologians—many from Latin America—reminded the Church that we need to practice what we preach. The Greek word for this is *orthopraxis,* which means "right acting," or "right doing." Jesus told us, "Not everyone who says to me, 'Lord, Lord,' shall enter the kingdom of heaven, but he who *does the will* of my Father" (Mt 7:21). God will judge us as sheep or as goats by how well we have fed the hungry, given drink to the thirsty, clothed the naked, and visited those in prison. When we do this for those who suffer, we do it for Jesus.

We also need to bring to this interplay between orthodoxy and orthopraxis still another notion, the Greek word *orthopathy,* which means "right feeling." Right thinking and right doing come together in right feeling. We should "feel" with the Church as well as think and act with her. We need to know her heart. This is where the notion of the Church as our mother becomes so fruitful. The Church is much more our mother than our father. We use the word "mother" to describe the Church because the Church is our home, and mothers make a home in a way fathers never will, even if they care for the children and the mother works outside the home. The Church is the place where we draw nourishment, just as we received nourishment at our mother's breast when we were children. It is therefore vital that we feel with the Church—that we know her heart.

A story captures this. A theologian is walking along the shore of the ocean. He sees a young girl flying a kite. The day is overcast, and he can't see the kite because of the clouds. He says to the girl, "Well, how do you know the kite's really there?" She answers him, "I can feel the tug of it." That's where the truth is found. As we search for God's truth, we discover it as we *feel* it with the Church. We feel the tug of it, the tug of the truth.

I suggested earlier that a cultural war is taking place throughout American society today, from the definition of marriage to gun control, capital punishment, and abortion. The Church urgently needs to engage our culture, and each of us individually needs to do the same. Christian faith requires from us a habit of connecting the gospel to daily life, and anchoring daily life in the gospel. That's what a dialogue with the world is really about. A constant exchange should occur between the gospel and our lives. This should happen not only as individuals, but also as a society.

We also need to understand that the partners in this dialogue are not equal. In our personal dialogue with the gospel, the gospel stands in judgment on us, because the gospel is the Word of God. Likewise, in dialogue with the secular world, the world and the gospel are not equal partners. The gospel is a gift to us from God, and thus it carries an authority that the world utterly lacks. This is why our view of the gospel has huge implications. If we believe that Scripture is just the words of some very wise people, then Scripture can be changed, diluted, and made more convenient. Then the gospel, instead of the world, is transformed in the dialogue. We can never allow this to happen. The gospel stands in judgment on each of us. It also rightly stands in judgment on the world and society.

Dialogue can sometimes be a code word. Before I became a bishop, I served as a Capuchin provincial. I noticed that my brothers would occasionally say to me, after I asked them to take an assignment, that they wanted to "dialogue" about it. Of course, what they usually wanted was to talk me out of what I was asking them to do. Sometimes we use the term "dialogue" when we really just want to argue the other person into doing things our way. When your children say, "Let's talk about it," they actually mean they're going to try to change your mind.

Therefore, we shouldn't be misled by a false notion of "dialogue." After Vatican II, some of us in the Church were much too confident. We were greatly optimistic that, through our dialogue with the world, everyone would rush to kneel at the feet of Christ, and the world would be transformed. Decades have passed, and it hasn't happened. The problem isn't Vatican II, but rather the world. The world hasn't been an honest partner in dialogue, and dialogue, in and of itself, isn't our goal. The goal of authentic Christian dialogue with culture is incarnating God's truth. Much of secular culture simply isn't interested in authentic dialogue, either because it feels superior to the Church or because it doesn't want to risk feeling guilty.

After the 1999 shootings at Columbine High School, the bishops of Colorado discussed and reflected on Francis of Assisi in our private meetings. Francis' contemporaries called him the *vir Catolicus*, Latin for "Catholic man." Francis modeled how the gospel could be lived in every age through peacemaking, forgiveness, and reconciliation. Yet he also modeled preaching and teaching the truth without compromise. In his "Final Testament" to his brothers, Francis taught that part of conversion involves "leaving the world." He said, "I tarried for a little while, and then I *finally* left the world." Most of us are still tarrying. We haven't left the world, and we don't want to. We've partly embraced our Christian vocation, but we really haven't immersed ourselves in Jesus Christ. In fact, sometimes we belong more to the world than to the kingdom of God.

A while ago, a story appeared in a local Denver newspaper with the headline, "We're in the money and loving it." The sub-head read, "Wealth permeates all levels of America like never before." Another news story reported that the national weekly average for teenagers receiving an allowance had reached $50. I reread those stories before Christmas, when still other news media reported that Americans wanted more meaning and less "stuff" from the holiday season. But of course—exactly as in years past—we went out and spent an enormous amount of money on "stuff" anyway. We want things of lasting spiritual substance, but we like things that feel good and make us comfortable right now. Catholics revel in this contradiction just as eagerly as does the general culture. That's sad, because one of the unique things about our vocation as Christians is that it calls us to get serious about leaving the world for the sake of the world.

Leaving the world does not mean hating the world. St. Francis loved the world. He saw it as a gift of God. He was radically ascetical because he understood his own selfishness. Yet in the midst of his self-denial, he very much loved the world around him as an expression of God's beauty and loving design. This is why environmental groups that criticize Christianity for having an "exploitative" view of the world, and then promote St. Francis as an icon of ecology, simply know nothing about him. Francis loved the world because he loved Jesus Christ, because he loved the gospel, and because he loved the Church.

At the moment of his conversion, Francis heard a call from Jesus to rebuild the Church. When Francis rediscovered the gospel, he rediscovered the Church. Francis told his brothers to always be submissive and subject at the feet of the Church, and steadfast in their Catholic faith. So, too, for everyone who wants to follow Jesus Christ. If we truly wish to participate in the life of the community we call the Church, we need to stop thinking about the Church as if she were a political organization, social club, or corporation. We need to stop thinking like American consumers and lobbyists, and start thinking like Catholic believers.

Christians should be radical in their embrace of the gospel. That's what made Francis different from other reformers of his time. Many other reformers lived and worked during the lifetime of St. Francis, with many different agendas for solving the problems of the Church and the world. Some had as much talent as Francis, and some were more radical. Yet what set Francis apart was his relationship with the Church. He knew instinctively that we'd be much more faithful to our vocation as Christians if we were much more faithful to the Church.

As we've already seen, Francis insisted that his brothers follow the gospel *sine glossa*—without accommodation. He wanted no explaining away of the meaning of Scripture. As Francis saw it, Jesus said what He intended, and therefore to follow the gospel was not confusing. It was difficult to be faithful—but it wasn't complicated. That was the magic of Francis. He wanted to rediscover the gospel, and to live it plainly and simply—without gloss.

All of us are required, if we're going to be faithful Christians, to embrace the gospel and the Church for what they are, not for what we'd prefer them to be. That means rediscovering and participating in the Church without gloss, without putting certain teachings in parentheses, or making exceptions for ourselves.

The Church does need our criticism, and quite honestly welcomes it. As a bishop, I need to hear what people really think about everything. We should *never* be afraid of questioning and criticism in the Church. Yet this should always be done with the same respect we show in questioning or criticizing someone we love. Criticism motivated by love doesn't stir up rebellion, and it doesn't break family unity. The Church is always in need of reform—but our call to reform has to be filled with respect and affection.

We must recommit our lives to the task of evangelizing the nations of the earth. As John Paul II has said, "it is not permissible for anyone to remain idle." We are called to the vineyard, to the world around us, nourished by a deeper life within the Church. If we're faithful to that call, we can have the same impact on our Church and on our world that Francis had in his time. So have confidence in your vocation. Be faithful to the Church. Through you, God will begin to change the world.

CHAPTER SEVEN

Building and Rebuilding Our Lives in Christ

Steve Martin has always been one of my favorite comedians. There's a skit he did on one of the old *Saturday Night Live* shows from the 1980s. He came out on stage. The lights were dimmed. Then he stepped into the spotlight and very piously began to recite a litany called "What I Believe." It went something like this:

"*I believe* that all of us are obligated to help the poor and unfortunate around the world ... unless they smell bad, or it's really inconvenient."

"And *I believe* that every man should worship in the church of his choice on Sunday ... unless there's a game on."

"And *I believe* in living my life by the Golden Rule and the Ten Commandments ... or at least eight of them."

And so on. Steve Martin's genius is that he makes us laugh at our own hypocrisies and excuses. He poked fun at the chasm between what we say we believe, and what we really believe, as evidenced by what we do.

What we say we believe needs to guide and rule everything

we do in life, or it isn't *really* what we believe. Over the last few chapters, we've been discussing the basics of Catholic belief—becoming a Christian, growing in Christ, living in Christ, and participating in the special community we call the Church. In this chapter, we need to look at living this Catholic life more deeply. We do this by using the road map that God has provided for us. Then we can move on to an examination of how we can repair and rebuild our life in Christ when sin begins to rule our actions.

Most of us know that a debate has been simmering over the Ten Commandments in recent years. We've seen battles in various states over posting the Ten Commandments in our public schools in order to discourage violence and build character. A judge in one state wants to post the Ten Commandments in his courtroom. His reasoning is that in his experience as a judge, he's found that many of the people who come before him in trouble have simply lost sight of God's basic laws. He therefore wants to post them for everyone to see and absorb. Of course, this has gotten him into trouble. Various people and "freedom from religion" groups claim that posting the Commandments constitutes the establishment of religion. Before it's over, the issue could go all the way to the Supreme Court. This is a pretty foolish waste of time and money, but that's the way things work today in our culture. We don't want to spend too much time here in a discussion of constitutional law, although we might note that the face of Moses is engraved inside the House of Representatives in Washington. Nobody has demanded that it be chiseled away, and it hasn't yet led to the destruction of the Republic.

Instead, let's focus on an interesting aspect of this debate that you might have missed. Some people have argued—in defense of the judge—that posting the Commandments has nothing to do with faith. They say that the Commandments are simply a compilation of rules for decent living that people of goodwill can agree upon in any society, whether they're lost in the Sinai Desert, or walking down the streets of Minneapolis. So, are the Ten Commandments merely a summary of human wisdom on how to get along? Were they created by men to give order to a society wandering in the desert?

We do believe the Ten Commandments make "common sense," but they make *common sense* because they're rooted in God's *common law*, the Natural Law, which guides and governs all peoples, in all times. They are more than just common sense. They're something much greater than a Top 10 list put together by Moses to keep his stiff-necked people from killing each other. In fact, there's a word we use to describe the extraordinary event that gave us the Ten Commandments. The word is *theophany*. It describes the actual appearance or manifestation of God.

The Ten Commandments were delivered to Moses in a theophany. It was a real event (witnessed, seen, and heard), in a real place (Mount Sinai), at a real time (after the Israelites departed from Egypt). The *Catechism of the Catholic Church* says that, "[The Commandments] belong to God's revelation of Himself and His glory. The gift of the Commandments is the gift of God Himself and His holy will. In making His will known, God reveals Himself to His people. The gift of the Commandments and of the Law is part of the covenant God sealed with His own" (2059).

The Ten Commandments are not man-made inventions. They come from God, and they express how we must live, since we belong to God. Yet there's more. The Ten Commandments not only reveal God. They are also part of God's revelation of who man is, a revelation that comes to full fruition in the person of Jesus Christ. Moral living conforms us to our God-given identity. It's our response to God's loving initiative. The Commandments, then, are our standards for living, and also the rules for our own spiritual health.

From at least the time of St. Augustine, in the fifth century, the Ten Commandments have held a predominant place in catechesis and moral instruction for the faithful. The first three commandments confirm our relationship with God. The fourth through the tenth commandments govern our relationship with our neighbors. While I'm sure you can recite them from memory, I'm going to list them anyway. Here's why. Some years ago a Dominican theologian whom I respect very much was teaching theology to students at an East Coast college. After a couple of years, he realized that in nearly every class he taught, students were unable to list accurately the Ten Commandments or the Seven Sacraments. That included students who had gone through twelve years of Catholic education. So now he takes nothing for granted—and neither should we.

The Ten Commandments are traditionally summarized from Scripture as follows:

I am the Lord your God: you shall not have strange gods before me. We begin with the most fundamental acknowledgement of faith: God exists. How often we live out our days forgetting that singular premise: God exists. The first commandment gives

God's first requirement of us: that we accept Him, accept His fatherly authority over our lives, and worship Him, because He is the source of our being.

The second part of this first commandment reminds us not to put anything ahead of God. Certainly, this refers to superstition or putting our trust in horoscopes. Yet it means much more than that. It means living our lives by making God first. Gayle Sayers, Hall-of-Fame running back for the Chicago Bears, wrote a little biography that he called "I Am Third." In his life, he wrote, God comes first, and his family second. Gayle Sayers comes third.

We ignore this commandment when we put the world— careers, money, power, sex, pleasure, all the little "gods" that distract us from God—ahead of God. We don't have to worship a golden calf in our backyard to be missing the meaning of this commandment. When we put the things of the world ahead of God, we're putting foreign gods before Him.

You shall not take the name of the Lord your God in vain. Each of our names is a sacred thing. The name we receive at Baptism is the name by which we will be called for all eternity. The names of God, of Jesus, of Mary, and of the saints, therefore, are names not to be invoked lightly. The second commandment warns us against perjury, false or inconsequential oaths, and blasphemy. But again, these things are obvious. The commandment also, more fundamentally, reminds us of the reality of the sacred— and our obligation to honor those things that are holy. If our culture has lost anything in recent years, it's a sense of awe in the presence of that which is holy. "Is nothing sacred?" is a common complaint today for a very good reason. Hundreds of things are politically correct, but virtually nothing is sacred. That's the difference between a consensus and revealed faith. This commandment reminds us that God is sacred and that the name of God, as John Cardinal Newman told us, should be on our lips only to bless, praise, and glorify Him.

Remember to keep holy the Lord's Day. "This is the day which the Lord has made," the psalmist sang, "Let us rejoice and be glad in it." In Jewish tradition, the Sabbath is a day of rest from work, set aside for prayer, worship, and remembrance of the covenant between God and His people. Justin Martyr, a second-century Father of the Church, explained the Christian celebration of the Lord's Day to the Romans: "We gather on the day of the sun, for it is the first day when God, separating matter from darkness, made the world; and on this day Jesus Christ our Savior, rose from the dead."

The third commandment's requirement to keep the Lord's Day holy centers, for Catholics, on the celebration of the Eucharist. It's a law of the Church that the faithful are obligated to participate in Mass on Sundays, or on the evening preceding Sunday. As much as possible, the Church strongly encourages us to keep the Lord's Day holy in the traditional manner: refraining from work, using our time for worship and prayer, performing works of mercy, and setting aside time for rest, relaxation, and meditation. In today's culture, it has become more and more difficult to keep Sunday as a day of rest. Many are required to work in order to provide for their families. It's a curious judgment on our times that in a culture so devoted to consumption and leisure, a day for worship and genuine rest has become impossible for so many.

Recently, the bishops of the Denver province issued a pastoral statement that reminds all our people that "Sunday worship—and by extension, worship on all days that the Church designates as 'holy'—is never merely an optional matter. It is an act of praise and thanksgiving, community and solidarity, vital to the health of the whole Church." The bishops further stressed that "worship is a form of witness ... and by our witness, we 'make disciples of all nations.'" Sunday is not just a day for TV and shopping. The Holy Father calls Sunday the "weekly Easter," and "the soul of all other days." If we believe in Jesus Christ and the Church He founded, then we need to conform our hearts and our actions to what Christ's Church teaches. That means recovering the holiness of Sunday.

Incidentally, a sign I once saw remains in my memory. It was standing in front of a pond at a small Christian college. It read, "No fishing on Sunday." While I admire the sentiment for keeping the Lord's Day, I'd be hard pressed to find a better example of what Jesus meant when He reminded us that the Sabbath was made for man, not man for the Sabbath. Enshrined in the Commandments is God's desire for us to rest and enjoy His creation. I wouldn't rule out a little fishing, but then I'm a fisherman, both by vocation and by hobby. Even some golf wouldn't be too bad—but after Mass.

Honor your father and your mother. In the fourth commandment, God blesses the family as a community of faith, hope, and charity, a "domestic Church." In the *Catechism of the Catholic Church* we read that "God has willed that, after Him, we should honor our parents to whom we owe life and who have handed on to us the knowledge of God" (2197).

While this commandment seems to be directed primarily toward children, it assumes the duties of parents in raising children in the light of faith. Parents share in the Lord's work of creation through procreation. Through example, education, and a home built on the foundations of prayer, fidelity to God, respect, and caring for one another, parents educate children in the faith. They evangelize a new generation. As children become adults, respect replaces obedience. Moreover, the duty to honor our parents never ends, and it extends to caring for them when the time might come, through illness or aging, when they will rely on our support as we once relied on theirs.

You shall not kill. This is the fifth commandment, and it has made the Church a sign of contradiction in our time. It's utterly straightforward: Do not kill. Yet we tend to want to make it gray. Do not kill, unless we're talking about "fetuses," which is a medical term used in order to draw attention away from the fact that fetuses are unborn children. Do not kill, unless we're talking about the severely disabled. Do not kill, unless we're talking about criminals. Do not kill, unless we're talking about our enemies. Do not kill, unless we're talking about the terminally sick, the aged, and the infirm. Our society puts more and more conditions on what constitutes a worthwhile life. We qualify and quantify life on the basis of utility, rather than a God-given sacredness.

The teaching of this commandment is very clear. It underlies every Catholic position on the life issues, and the entire social doctrine of the Church. Human life is sacred because it comes from God. In the *Catechism of the Catholic Church,* we read: "Every human life, from the moment of conception until death, is sacred because the human person has been willed for its own sake in the image and likeness of the living and holy God" (2319). This is the foundation stone of John Paul II's great 1995 encyclical *The Gospel of Life*. But it also anchors every other great Catholic social justice teaching document in the last one hundred years, from *Rerum Novarum* through *Pacem in Terris* to *Sollicitudo Rei Socialis*.

You shall not commit adultery. It's this commandment, the sixth, which commits us to chastity. That's an old word with a wealth of meaning. When we think of chastity, we often equate it with virginity, or sexual abstinence. Yet it's much more than that. It involves the integrity of the person, and how sexuality is expressed in a relationship between two people. Living a chaste life means ridding ourselves of a particular and very powerful form of selfishness. Chastity means not using others as objects of sexual satisfaction, either by our actions or in our thoughts. Chastity is a gift from God, and it comes from sustained spiritual effort and from grace.

From this commandment, the Church unfolds her teaching on human sexuality. This teaching, like Catholic teaching on the life issues, is centered on the sacredness of each human person. The pornography we find so widespread on the Internet, in our movies and popular music, and even on prime-time television is not just a private diversion. It has very big public consequences in contraception, abortion, prostitution, marital breakup, and the sexual abuse of women and children. More than half of all sites on the Internet are pornography-oriented. Anyone who claims that this doesn't have a massive social impact is either confused or deliberately evading the truth.

You shall not steal. The seventh commandment forbids the taking of our neighbor's goods. That means everything from stealing money to padding our expenses to cheating on college exams. All of these involve a kind of theft. We all know what theft is, and we all know it's wrong. Yet there's more to this commandment as well. Through the centuries, particularly since the nineteenth century, the Church has applied this commandment to the dignity of work. Work is an honorable thing. In fact, it's a duty. Paul admonished the Thessalonians that if a member of the community refused to work he should not be allowed to eat. Yet, work is for man, not man for work. Through this commandment, the Church focuses on the rights of the worker to a decent wage and the honorable working conditions that allow for a family to be raised in a healthy and holy atmosphere. To do otherwise is to steal from the worker.

It's this commandment that mandates that the Church make a preferential option for the poor. The great Eastern Father of the Church, St. John Chrysostom, warned us centuries ago that "Not to enable the poor to share in our goods is to steal from them and deprive them of life. The goods we possess are not ours, but theirs."

You shall not bear false witness against your neighbor. The eighth commandment asks us to live in truth. As Jesus admonished the apostles, "Let what you say be simply 'Yes' or 'No'" (Mt 5:37). Yet this commandment also requires that we seek the truth, and then bear witness to the truth. It demands that we be persons of integrity, and "integrity" comes from the Latin word for being whole or complete. The truth makes us whole by making us morally complete.

Of course, our world today is caught up in the same question that Pilate derisively asked Jesus: "Truth? What does that mean?" It has become virtually the definition of modernity to deny that permanent, objective truth exists apart from opinion. Everything is relative. No objective reality exists outside our own perceptions and interpretations. Yet the statement of Jesus is clear: "For this was I born, and for this have I come into the world, to bear witness to the truth. Every one who is of the truth hears my voice" (Jn 18:37). What the Church has taught, consistently and always, is that truth exists apart from us. It exists, whether we believe it or not. The eighth commandment tells us that we must find that truth in Jesus, we must speak that truth in Jesus, and we must spread that truth in His name.

You shall not covet your neighbor's wife. The ninth commandment calls us to Christian purity of heart, body, and faith. In the Sermon on the Mount, Jesus preached, "Blessed are the pure in heart, for they shall see God." The *Catechism of the Catholic Church* summarizes it especially well: "The 'pure in heart' are promised that they will see God face-to-face and be like Him. Purity of heart is the precondition of the vision of God. Even now it enables us to see according to God, to accept others as 'neighbors'; it lets us perceive the human body—ours and our neighbor's—as a temple of the Holy Spirit, a manifestation of divine beauty" (2519).

You shall not covet your neighbor's goods. One of the emptiest posters I've ever seen is the one that proclaims, "Whoever dies with the most toys, wins!" It's common to the human condition that we want things we don't have. The tenth commandment completes the ninth commandment, reminding us that envy, greed, and avarice should be banished from the Christian life. It also reminds us that the willful desire or intent for an evil action is as wrong as the action itself. What resides in our hearts, counts.

It's ironic. Many of us spend a good deal of our lives accumulating stuff. What the "stuff" is will differ from person to person. Yet at the end of our lives, it's all finally the same junk. It piles up in bookcases, in garages, in boxes in the attic, in the secret places of our souls. As life's evening sets in, we see the need to begin to detach. The things we've accumulated are distractions. They should become less and less important. We need to strip them away—the layers of our life—until, at the very end, all that is left is God and us. "Blessed are the poor in spirit, for theirs is the kingdom of heaven" (Mt 5:3). Thus, I suspect that poster—"Whoever dies with the most toys, wins"—should really read, "Whoever dies with *no toys*, wins."

Jesus summarized the commandments for us in this way: "You shall love the Lord your God with all your heart, with all your soul, with all your mind, and with all your strength [and] you shall love your neighbor as yourself" (Mk 12:30-31). When we live our lives in violation of the commandments, we undermine our friendship with God and with our neighbors.

There's been a trend in some schools of moral theology over the years to paint the commandments as the Ten Suggestions. The reason the Steve Martin skit was so funny on *Saturday Night Live* is because it's uncomfortably true. Many of us prefer to see the teachings of the Church as worthy goals. We like to think they're not binding, because we delude ourselves into believing that they're not "realistic." Sure, we should keep them in mind, but only saints can truly live up to them. So we can ignore or bend them when we need to. We apply a little, or a lot, of that gloss that St. Francis warned his followers about. The trouble is, nothing in Jesus' words or actions supports that kind of mental laziness. Hell is certainly going to be very "realistic" if we end up there.

Jesus will forgive even the worst sinner if he or she is contrite. Zacchaeus, the tax collector, not only repented, he changed his life and made amends for his sins. That's the kind of honest, converted heart Jesus loves. Yet Jesus has very little use for the proud, the lazy, or the cynical. As we saw earlier, "sin" is a bad word these days, not because we don't believe in it, but because we don't want to believe in it. Therapy is a lot easier than repentance. Self-improvement is a lot less demanding than conversion. That's why Philip Rieff once described modern culture as "the triumph of the therapeutic." For millions of people today, the language of psychology has displaced the idea of sin, and therapy has made confession obsolete. Yet therapy on its own can never address—much less deliver us from—the mystery of evil. The twentieth century was a catalogue of the consequences not of social or psychological inadequacies, *but of sin*. World wars, abortion on demand, the Holocaust, poverty, mass hunger, ethnic cleansing—the list of tragedies is long. God doesn't rejoice in such horror. Mankind creates it by its own sinfulness.

Let's not focus only on the big story, however. We can easily point to Hitler, Stalin, or Pol Pot and their crimes against humanity and condemn them as great sinners. Their sins make the transgressions of everyday life seem like small change. Yet, as Paul told the Romans, "None of us lives to himself, and none of us dies to himself" (14:7). The sins of our own lives, no matter how private or public, affect everything around us. There may be lonely sinners, but there are no lonely sins.

Here's just one example from a story played out over a number of years. It was probably twenty-five years ago when a young man cheated on his wife. She found out and had her own affair with another married man, for no other reason than to get even with her husband for his infidelity. That affair was found out as well. All those involved decided to put it behind them and start again. Except they couldn't. It didn't work. An illness had entered the two marriages. Eventually, both couples divorced. The first wife never remarried, and struggled to raise two children on her own. One child ended up healthy and happy, while the other turned into a continuing problem. Her husband eventually ruined his career, then ruined a second marriage. The other husband and wife divorced as well, and their children bore the brunt of it. As young adults, two of their children have already been in and out of marriage, putting their own children at risk. You've probably seen similar stories yourself.

One "little" affair more than two decades ago, and the ripples still haven't subsided. People are still paying the price, and innocent and not-so-innocent lives have never been the same, all because of one sin, committed in a rush of ego and desire.

Sin involves more, of course, than even the human wreckage so obvious to all of us. Because of our unity in Christ, every sin affects the life of all of us in the Church. Paul wrote to the Corinthians (1 Cor 12:26-27), "If one member suffers, all suffer together. If one member is honored, all rejoice together. Now you are the body of Christ and individually members of all." As the *Catechism of the Catholic Church* explains, "In this solidarity with all men, living or dead, which is founded on the communion of saints, the least of our acts done in charity redounds to the profit of all. Every sin harms this communion" (953).

There's an old book by Myles Connolly called *Mr. Blue*. I'm not even sure if it's still in print. But you might be able to find it in a used bookstore, or on the Internet. It's a simple but profound little book you can read in an evening. Mr. Blue is a will-o'-the-wisp kind of fellow, a modern St. Francis. At one point, Blue describes the epitaph he would like on his headstone: "The other day I was thinking of what people would say when I'm dead. So, I thought I would leave them a line for my grave. That is, if I have a grave. I don't care one way or another. But I do wish someone would write these lines about me somewhere:

> 'Never was there a worse sinner,
> And never was God kinder to one.'"

Talk of sin—and acknowledging our own sinfulness—should never lead to despair. "By despair," the *Catechism of the Catholic Church* teaches, "man ceases to hope for his personal salvation from God, for help in attaining it, or for the forgiveness of sins. Despair is contrary to God's goodness, to His justice—for the Lord is faithful to his promises—and to His mercy" (2091).

God is all-merciful. His kindness extends beyond the bounds of the universe, and to the smallest corner of our souls. Catherine of Siena described the mercy of God in a prayer: "The mercy which pours forth from you fills the whole world. It was by your mercy that we were created, and by your mercy that you redeemed us by sending your Son. Your mercy is the light in which sinners find you and good people come back to you. Your mercy is everywhere...."

God calls us to repent of our sins and to seek forgiveness. Through the Sacrament of Penance, we meet God as our merciful Father. Through this sacrament, we're reconciled with God and the Church. Yet there's more. So many of our sins involve hurting others. The two great commandments require that we love God and our neighbor. As we seek reconciliation with God and His Church, we must also learn to ask for forgiveness, to make amends for what we have done to others, and to grant forgiveness to those who have hurt us. This is the foundation of a vibrant spiritual life and a soul on fire with faith.

It's a curious thing that in an age of vast spiritual hunger, we've witnessed a diminishing reception of the Sacrament of Penance. I've often wondered about the reasons for the decline. It certainly isn't caused by our greater saintliness. Let me point out two clues: The first is rationalization. Even when we acknowledge the existence of sin, we can reason it away in our own lives. We find a thousand alibis to explain away our wrongdoing. In the old movie *The Big Chill*, one character says that rationalization is our single greatest necessity. You can go a day without food, without water, without just about anything, the character says. But try getting through a day without at least one rationalization for bad behavior.

The second clue is old-fashioned hubris. It hurts our pride to examine our sins, admit them for what they are—without excuses—and seek forgiveness. It's not in our nature to be humble. It's not in our nature to acknowledge that we've done wrong. It's all just a little embarrassing.

Yet, for those who frequent the Sacrament regularly, it's a cause for neither embarrassment nor hurt pride. It's a celebration—a liberation—from the chains that hold us down. We can feel in our souls a new freedom from the sins that once held us in bondage, and a reconciliation with God and with His Church. A writer, fallen away from the Church, once described the sacramental confessions of his youth in a humorous way. Yet after each confession, he admitted, "I felt free. Free! Free! Free!—a glorious freedom from sin that made the day look bright and the world look good. I've never felt that way since."

Receiving the sacrament is so very simple that it should be a regular part of every healthy spiritual life. We start with a personal examination of conscience, looking inward to review what we've done and what we've failed to do since our last Confession. We begin our Confession with the Sign of the Cross, and the priest might provide a brief reading from Scripture on the mercy of God and the need for repentance. We then confess our sins, and the priest offers advice, counsel, and a suitable penance. We express in an Act of Contrition our sorrow for our sins: "Lord Jesus, Son of God, have mercy on me, a sinner."

The priest then speaks the words of absolution: "God, the Father of mercies, through the death and resurrection of His Son has reconciled the world to Himself and sent His Holy Spirit among us for the forgiveness of sins; through the ministry of the Church, may God give you pardon and peace, and I absolve you from your sins in the name of the Father, and of the Son, and of the Holy Spirit."

And we are free. Free. *Free.*

CHAPTER EIGHT

Finding Our Vocation

Cheech and Chong had a stand-up comedy routine years ago, and in it they'd pretend to be in a classroom at the beginning of the school year. One of them would read the essay we all had to write for homework every September, "How I Spent My Summer Vacation." The essay went something like this:

> How I Spent My Summer Vacation. The first day I got up, had breakfast, then went out to look for a job. Nobody was hiring. Then I spent the rest of the day hanging around in front of the drugstore. The next day, I got up, had breakfast, then went out to look for a job. Nobody was hiring. Then I spent the rest of the day hanging around in front of the drugstore. The next day, I got up, had breakfast, then went out to look for a job. Then I got a job—keeping kids from hanging out in front of the drugstore. The End.

Remember the first jobs we all had? No, not delivering the morning paper, babysitting, or mowing the neighbor's lawn for a few dollars. I mean those first real, full-day jobs for a paycheck. We all know a lawyer who worked as a fish cutter; a truck dealer who got his first paycheck as a chicken packer; a construction worker who started out as a theatre usher.

Whenever I raise the subject of a first job, a similar theme runs through every person's experience. The work was grueling, the pay was low, and an unpleasant boss usually made life difficult. Yet, no matter how tough the job—no matter how hard or sweaty—people take a certain odd pride in it. A man might have spent four decades as a leading banker, but he'll wax poetic about the summer he worked the docks down by the river. A successful woman surgeon will recall with a smile the year she spent selling encyclopedias door-to-door.

We're often schizophrenic about our work. We tend to define who we are by what we do; yet we also imagine our working lives as something completely distinct from who we are. Work is where we play life's game by a different set of rules, which have little to do with what we really value. The shop is usually the first place where we leave our faith at the door. A reporter once asked a prominent Catholic businessman about the moral implications of closing down a plant and putting people out of work. "That's business," he shrugged. "It has nothing to do with my religion."

All of us share that attitude from time to time. We take our work, box it up, and put it in a corner. We rarely perceive our work as playing any major role in our spiritual lives or in our responsibilities as members of the body of Christ. Yet most of our waking moments are spent on the job, and if our faith doesn't apply there, it can't have much practical effect on our lives.

When we use the word "vocation" in Catholic circles, we often think of a call to the priesthood or religious life, but in fact it means much more. "Vocation" involves keeping house, raising kids, banging out letters on a word processor, hauling garbage, teaching school, selling shoes, practicing law, covering city hall, and making loans. Vocation can be the length and breadth of any life lived for God. The faith and Christian commitment we bring to our work make it our vocation.

Jim Davidson, a Catholic sociologist from the Midwest, has done some interesting studies on faith and work. In one survey he asked average persons like you and me whether we think of our work as a job, a career, or a calling. He defined a "job" as a service we're paid to perform. We might like it or dislike it. We've been paid to do other things, and we're more than willing to do something else if better pay or better security comes with it. A *career*, he said, is another matter. This is where we pick a particular field and plan to pursue it as our life's work: a veterinarian, let's say, or a computer programmer. We might work for different people or companies over time, but we'll stay in the same profession.

Then there are those for whom work is a calling, a *vocation*. These people, Davidson wrote, believe that God has called them specifically to do the work they accomplish. Their work becomes a way to glorify God, no matter what that task might involve. They believe God created them to cooperate in His work, and they will do so no matter how much, or little, they're compensated.

When Davidson surveyed a group of affluent church congregations—both Protestant and Catholic—he found that about half the people viewed their work as a career. Another 29 percent viewed their work as a "job"—something they did to earn a paycheck. Only about 15 percent considered their work to be a calling.

Interestingly, Davidson's study showed that for people who saw their work as a calling, education, salary, and perks didn't really matter. The only real variable among those who had a calling and those who had a career or a job was faith. "The more important religion was to people, and the more religiously active they were," Davidson reported, "the more likely they were to think of their work as a calling.... The key factor that separated people who saw their work as a calling was religious commitment—the tendency to think of religion as an important part of one's life, and to act accordingly, both in church and in the world."

Our work—whatever it is—should become a means to pursue holiness for ourselves and for our families, and to model holiness to those around us. The *Catechism of the Catholic Church* explains that

> Human work proceeds directly from persons created in the image of God and called to prolong the work of creation by subduing the earth, both with and for one another.... Work honors the Creator's gifts and the talents received from Him. It can also be redemptive. By enduring the hardship of work in union with Jesus, the carpenter of Nazareth and the one crucified on Calvary, man collaborates in a certain fashion with the Son of God in His redemptive work. He shows himself to be a disciple of Christ by carrying the cross, daily, in

the work he is called to accomplish. Work can be a means of sanctification.... (2427)

In a successful market economy, of course, it can become very difficult to separate the real human value of work from the financial rewards that the market assigns—or withholds. Few people will ever get rich teaching in a Catholic school, for example, but the enduring value of their work outweighs most of the earnings on Wall Street.

The idea of "vocation" reminds us that life has a purpose, and more urgently, *that our lives have purpose.* Happiness consists not in accumulating money or things, but in discovering and pursuing the path God intends for us. In Charles Dickens' *The Christmas Carol,* the ghost of Jacob Marley offers a powerful and troubling vision to the old miser, Ebenezer Scrooge. As dead souls weep over a starving and impoverished young woman and her child, alone in the snow of a London alley, Scrooge asks, "Why do they lament so?" Marley answers, "Because they seek to intercede for good in human affairs, and have lost the ability to do so." Time is precious. Life is shorter than we think, and none of us has any guarantee that we'll have a chance tomorrow to do the good things we neglect today. Morever, the good we can accomplish in this life is not just a "duty." It's a privilege we receive through the grace of Baptism and the help of the Holy Spirit.

The gifts of the Holy Spirit provide us with the strength and courage to show God alive in our lives, as He works through us to lead others to Christ and to renew the face of the world. Traditionally, the Church has listed these gifts as wisdom, understanding, counsel, fortitude, knowledge, piety, and fear of the Lord. These seven "gifts of the Holy Spirit" lead us to become people who embody the twelve "fruits of the Holy Spirit"—charity, joy, peace, patience, kindness, goodness, generosity, gentleness, faithfulness, modesty, self-control, and chastity.

Through these gifts, and the fruits that flow from them in our own lives, we can follow our calling in the work we do each day, in our families and friendships, in our everyday encounters. We can commit ourselves daily to evangelization, to performing works of mercy, and to working to bring about a greater good in our wider community.

A lay friend of mine sometimes talks about the "cocktail evangelization circuit" his job routinely keeps him on. He explained that for many years he dreaded the social hours that play a key part of his business life. It wasn't just the watered-down scotch, he said, or the small talk that got smaller and smaller. His problem was that everyone knew he was a serious Catholic, and he found himself becoming an uncomfortable defender of the faith. At every cocktail party, someone would come after him. Ex-Catholics, nonbelievers, fundamentalists—someone always challenged his faith and asked questions. Sometimes people would take him aside, asking for counsel and advice. All this, he said, began to become too burdensome. He felt unworthy and unprepared.

Then, one day, he ran into a casual acquaintance from the business world. The man stopped and thanked him. "Yeah," the fellow told him, "I hadn't been square with the Church for a long time. I had drifted away. We were talking about it one night at a party for a few minutes. You got me thinking. My wife and I talked some things out, and we've been getting involved again in the Church. Things look a lot better. I just wanted to let you know that you made a difference." He shook my friend's hand and walked away. To this day, my friend can't remember talking to the man in the first place. But he's patiently worked the "cocktail evangelization circuit" ever since.

All of us evangelize. We evangelize our families and friends, our neighbors and our business associates. Parents evangelize their children. The faith begins in the family, and this is how most of us first learn of our baptismal responsibilities. Evangelization through parents never ends. They often teach us as much about the faith at the end of their lives as they do when we're young. They often *continue* to teach us through our memories, long after they've gone home to the Lord.

Yet most of our days are spent in more indirect witness: how we speak, how we live, the example we set to people we encounter. We set an example in everything we do, though we may never know the results, this side of heaven. For every conversion, for every life that turns to Christ, a silent evangelizer, known only to God and the convert, has done his or her quiet work.

We also evangelize through our prayers. Our participation in the Mass and the sacraments, the prayers we offer for those around us, our daily practice of the faith—all these quiet actions speak to an unbelieving world. Thus, the Church calls us to the *spiritual* works of mercy: counseling the doubtful, instructing the ignorant, admonishing the sinner, comforting the afflicted, forgiving offenses, bearing wrongs patiently, praying for the living and the dead. She also calls us to the *corporal* works of mercy: feeding the hungry, giving drink to the thirsty, clothing the naked, visiting the imprisoned, sheltering the homeless, visiting the sick, burying the dead.

We evangelize—or don't—by the movies we see, the videos we rent, the television we watch, the books and newspapers we read, the products we buy, the technology we use, the letters we write, the schools we create, the radio programs we choose, the museums we visit, the politics we support, the laws we pass. For good or ill, our habits help shape the culture that surrounds us and that bombards us every day with a thousand messages telling us how to think and feel, what to buy and what to eat, how to live and how to love.

We need a new examination of conscience today. We need to look critically at how many of our actions result from submitting the world to our faith ... and how many from submitting our faith to the world. How many of our conscious—and unconscious—activities stem from an unending propaganda blitz by a skeptical and unbelieving culture? How have we arrived at our views on capital punishment? Do they really reflect our faith in the sacredness of human life as taught by the Church? If not, why not?

Two final thoughts on the meaning of vocation.

First, from the time we're old enough to think about the future, each of us tends to ask: What do I want to be when I grow up? What do I want to do with the rest of my life? These are sensible, universal questions. But on a deeper level, they're also the wrong ones. Each of us has a purpose in this world. Each of us has a "calling." Finding our vocation requires that we listen for God's voice. It means asking: What does God want me to be when I "grow up?" What does God want me to do with the rest of my life?

Second, while the Lord calls each of us to follow Him in some unique form of service, the priesthood, in a very powerful way, plays a vital role for the whole People of God. As the Curé of Ars explained, the priest, configured to Christ by ordination, sacrificially "continues the work of redemption on earth," for the benefit of all believers and the entire world. God asks each of us—priests and lay alike—to help young men and women listen to His voice in their lives. In fact, a key part of our own vocation is to encourage vocations to the priesthood and religious life. God has appointed us mentors to the next generation of faith, and we mentor by our prayer, our example, our encouragement, and our personal support.

CHAPTER NINE

The Family as Leaven

L et's begin with a fable. We'll call it "A Tale of Two Movies." And let's call the movies Film A and Film B. They have a lot in common. Like every good fable, they teach a moral lesson.

Film A is about a married couple. They're young, talented, attractive, and they love each other very much. Both husband and wife have successful careers. Life is good. Then, one day, the wife gets sick, and she doesn't get better. In fact, no matter what her husband does to find a cure—and no matter how many doctors try to help—she gets worse. She starts to lose control of her muscles. Her pain goes from bad to worse. The wife is a very unselfish young woman. She can't bear the thought of becoming a burden to her husband. She also can't bear the thought of becoming ugly and a source of resentment in his life. So she asks him to help her end the suffering.

The young man loves his wife, so at first he resists. Eventually, however, he sees that the best way to love her is to help her die with dignity—and so he helps her commit suicide. Unfortunately, the young man lives in a country with very backward laws and very backward people who want to enforce those laws, so he's charged with homicide. Yet the young man is so decent, and the case for assisted suicide makes so much common sense, that the court finds him innocent. The inhumane laws are discredited, and so are the inhumane people who want to enforce them.

Now let's turn to Film B, about a boy who grows up in an orphanage. A wonderful, earthy, humane doctor runs the orphanage. The boy becomes his protégé and the son he never had. Over the years, the doctor teaches the boy all his medical skills. The boy becomes a gifted healer in his own right. Now, this doctor specializes in helping women who are pregnant and in trouble. One way he helps them is by delivering their babies and then providing the newborns with a loving home in the orphanage until someone adopts them. The other way this doctor helps is by doing illegal abortions. Unfortunately, some of the orphanage board members are narrow-minded and extremely religious, so he has to be very discreet. The doctor's young protégé has the job of burning the dead fetuses in the incinerator out back. Being an orphan himself, the boy refuses to take part in any of the abortions. Of course, he doesn't condemn the good doctor, but he won't perform the abortions himself.

Eventually the boy leaves the orphanage to make his way in the world. What he discovers is how terribly unjust the rules governing human behavior can be. When a young woman friend is raped and impregnated by her father, he realizes how selfish his scruples have been. He helps her by performing an abortion. Then he finds his way back to the orphanage, where he takes over the good work of his mentor.

Film A and Film B have a lot in common. In fact, they're cut from the same cloth. Both were major commercial films. Both were popular with general audiences. And both teach the same lesson: that traditional morality is the work of ignorant religious fanatics who don't care much about human suffering. The real humanists are people with enough compassion and courage to break the rules and defy moral convention.

Some of you might recognize Film B. It's *The Cider House Rules*. Michael Caine, the actor who played the abortionist, won an Academy Award for his role. Film A, however, may be a little harder to remember. Its title is *I Accuse*, and it was produced in Germany in 1941 to help justify the Third Reich's extermination campaign against the chronically ill and the mentally and physically handicapped.

Watching *The Cider House Rules* reminded me, in a strange way, of Tom Brokaw's best-selling book, *The Greatest Generation*, which is about the men and women who fought the Second World War to make it safe for Americans to live as a free people. It would be ironic, wouldn't it, if our country ended up becoming what our parents tried so hard to protect us from? Yet, it could happen, and in a way, it's already happening. I don't mean that we're becoming Nazis. We don't need to be that vulgar. We can lose our soul as a nation without supporting a lunatic ideology. We can lose our soul in a uniquely American way—by being selfish and pragmatic, by being faithless in our commitments, and by twisting our freedom into the right to do whatever we want. We don't even have to look very far for proof. The first cell of society is the family, and as the family goes, so goes the soul of the culture.

So, how goes the American family?

Today, only one in four American families can be described as intact and "traditional"—two parents, single income, with children living at home. This kind of family, which is more or less the classic American model, has declined by nearly half in less than thirty years. At the same time, the percentage of children living with single parents has quadrupled. Out-of-wedlock births occur far more frequently now than three decades ago. Divorce is much more widely accepted. Unmarried couples with no children make up one-third of all American households. In fact, they're now the largest single category of U.S. households.

The results shouldn't surprise us. Wounded families make a wounded culture. In fact, for more than a decade, social research has clearly shown that easy divorce and so-called diverse forms of family structure simply don't work. Stepparent and single-parent families do not reinforce our social fabric. Rather, they unintentionally weaken it, and they have a long-term effect. Children from broken families find it harder to build permanent marriages themselves. They have a tougher time excelling at school, avoiding crime, finding intimacy in relationships, and holding steady employment. Obviously, this isn't their fault, and none of these observations are meant as a criticism of the many good single-parent and blended families who struggle heroically to do the best they can. Yet the facts speak for themselves.

None of this information is new. None of it is secret. The only remarkable thing is how little sobering effect this knowledge has had on the unraveling of American family culture. The evidence hasn't changed anything. We know better, but too few people seem to care. Even when people do care, they can't agree on what to do about it. Meanwhile, even the legal definition of marriage continues to be challenged with initiatives like homosexual "civil unions."

The lesson here is simple. The day is gone when American Catholics could feel safe with the instincts of our public culture. We still think of ourselves as a more or less "Christian" people. More than 90 percent of Americans still pray and describe themselves as believing in God. American church attendance is still very high by Western standards. Yet the content of our experience has changed dramatically. Americans claim to be more "spiritual," but less formally religious. God, as *The New York Times* reported in 1997, has become "decentralized," because the "new breed of worshiper [looks] beyond the religious institution for a do-it-yourself solution."

What this means is fairly obvious. Communities of faith—which have the solidarity and resources to turn their moral beliefs into public influence—are slowly being replaced by unconnected individuals with looser spiritual yearnings. These are individuals who "want to reshape religion for themselves" and who experience God in a narrowly crafted, private way. As a result, the power that traditional Christian belief has always had in shaping American culture is quickly fading. With it goes the trust Americans once had that our civil environment would at least be neutral—if not friendly—to our faith. Fifty years ago abortion was a "crime against humanity" at the Nuremberg Trials. Even twenty years ago, a film like *The Cider House Rules* could not have been produced. Now the actor who played the abortionist wins an Oscar.

When John Paul II wrote in his *Letter to Families* in 1994, that "a civilization inspired by a consumerist, anti-birth mentality is not—and cannot ever be—a civilization of love" (13), he was probably talking about a country like ours, and the material comforts we take for granted. How do we change that? How do we build a civilization of love? First of all, by building a "family of families" within our own Church. We will either preach Jesus Christ and teach the Catholic faith to our surrounding culture together, or we will fail separately. Families have the mission of being a leaven of the gospel in the wider world. In fact, married life and parenting are missionary vocations.

In Mark's Gospel, Jesus appears to the eleven and tells them to "Go into all the world and preach the gospel to the whole creation" (Mk 16:15). Notice that Jesus didn't say, "proclaim the good news to all creation ... *unless you and your spouse are really busy.*" Notice that you don't need a theology degree, either. It can help, but it isn't necessary. The apostles Peter and John were "uneducated, common men," but they were bursting with the self-assurance and joy of faith: "for we cannot but speak of what we have seen and heard" (Acts 4:20). Faith demands to be shared, or it dies.

The Second Vatican Council said much the same thing in *Ad Gentes,* the *Decree on the Church's Missionary Activity.* The Council Fathers wrote that "the obligation of spreading the faith falls individually on every disciple of Christ" (23), and "the whole Church is missionary, and the work of evangelization [is] the fundamental task of the people of God" (35). Finally, they said, "all the faithful have an obligation to collaborate in the expansion and spread of [Christ's] body" (36).

How can a married couple, or a family with many responsibilities, really begin living as missionaries? I have two answers to that. First, I'd wager that God is right now calling some of the people reading these words to be active missionary families, either here in the United States among the poor, or in some other country. Is that really so outlandish? Not at all. Protestants have been doing it for years. In the Archdiocese of Denver alone, at least two foreign missionary families work among our people right now. One of the couples comes from the Christian Life Movement in Peru. They have young children and do wonderful work with our Hispanic people. The second couple has five children. They come from the Community of the Beatitudes in France, and they help prepare our people for marriage.

Both of these families left their friends and their homes behind. Both came to Colorado to "preach the good news to all creation," and both are succeeding. So, going to the missions as a couple or as a family is not impossible. Or rather, it's only impossible if you never listen for God's call. The opportunities exist if you look for them, especially in the many renewal movements and apostolic groups that have broken out all over the world since Vatican II. The Neocatechumenal Way, to cite just one example, has families on mission in countries all over the world.

Of course, going on mission implies a community effort. Every missionary family lives on faith—faith in God and faith in the people who support them in their work. Every missionary family needs three things: prayers, friendship, and material support. For every one family that goes on a mission, ten families could tithe to support them. That's not a burden. In fact, it's a gift to the families who stay behind. By their support, they take a direct hand in spreading the gospel.

Why is that important? *Because souls depend on it.* Because converting the world to Jesus Christ matters urgently and eternally. The salvation of individuals, cultures, and the world depends on it.

Here's the second answer to that question of how a family can actually begin to live as missionaries. Many families are struggling just to meet the demands of daily life. Raising a family is heroic work. God *isn't* calling most of you to move to Zimbabwe with your Bible. Yet you still have the duty to preach Jesus Christ to the world. How do you do that? Here's a clue, and it comes again from Vatican II's *Decree on the Church's Missionary Activity:* "let everyone be aware that the primary and most important contribution he [or she] can make to the spread of the faith is to lead a profound Christian life" (36). In other words, living the gospel ardently where you are is a form of missionary witness. Living the teachings of the Church joyfully and loyally *in the specific circumstances of your life* is missionary.

That's why a frail French nun in a cloister can become a doctor of the Church. That's why St. Thérèse of Lisieux is one of the great missionaries of all time. She never went to the missions. Instead, she brought the missions to her cloister by including the whole world in her prayers. She radiated Jesus Christ to the women with whom she lived, day in and day out, in a way that converted their hearts. If Thérèse could evangelize all alone from behind the walls of a convent, surely a married couple can evangelize their children, their friends, their coworkers, and their political environment.

Here's a simple question: Have you consciously tried to bring someone outside your immediate family into the Catholic Church in the last year? If you haven't, you're hurting your own faith by preventing Jesus from reaching others through you. Do you talk about God with your spouse, your children, your family? Do you worship as a family every Sunday? It's common for teachers in our own Catholic schools to tell me that as many as half of their students don't attend Sunday Mass regularly. That's in our *Catholic* schools, where tuition can be expensive. So we have a contradiction. Some Catholic parents—in fact, too many Catholic parents—are willing to sacrifice part of their income to get a good moral education for their children, but then they don't follow it up in the home with prayer, discussion, and regular participation in the Liturgy. *Yet that's where the really crucial Catholic education always takes place.* Without living the faith in the home, these children grow up, enter society as citizens, and don't understand why a movie like *The Cider House Rules* is essentially just propaganda for killing unborn children.

God ordained the family as the place where the life of Christ, life in abundance, takes root in the human heart and spreads outward to embrace the world. God ordained the family to mirror His own love, the community of love within the Trinity, and to be the school of love that soul by soul, generation by generation, builds up the Church and advances her work of salvation.

The Second Vatican Council said that pursuing our common missionary vocation requires us to live a "profound Christian life." For families, that means committing yourselves to the particular vocation of marriage and the family. The Church has plenty of resources to help you achieve that. Furthermore, since you're reading this little book, you already know the impor- tance of reading as a tool for growth in your faith.

I'm going to tell you about two documents. My advice is that you not only read them but pray over them. Discuss them. Get to know them intimately. Peter and John may have been "uneducated, common men" when they began their ministry, but they didn't stay that way. They matured into serious leaders— and so must you. Your faith should be cultivated and deepened throughout your life. That's part of our duty as adult Catholics. We should never stop learning about our faith.

So, first, read John Paul II's 1981 document *On the Family; Familiaris Consortio* is the Latin title. It describes marriage as the beginning and basis of human society. It describes the family as the first and vital cell of society. It also shows why the family cannot be an escape or an "enclave," and cannot avoid an active role in humanizing and Christianizing civil culture. The pope writes that, "It is from the family that citizens come to birth, and it is within the family that they find the first school of the social virtues which are the animating principle of the existence and development of society itself" (42). In other words, the family is powerful. By its nature, the family greatly influences those issues that are most intimate to civil society. Therefore, any attempt to "redefine" the family, or to disconnect the family from the social regulation of porno- graphy, abortion, homosexual behavior, and similar issues, inevitably damages civil society.

The second document builds on the first. In his 1994 *Letter to Families,* John Paul II writes, "A truly sovereign and vigorous nation is always made up of strong families who are aware of their vocation and mission in history" (17). He goes on to say, "how indispensable is the witness of all families who live their vocation day by day [and] how urgent it is for families to pray" (5). Why? Because "the family is the center and the heart of the civilization of love," and "only if the truth about freedom and the communion of persons in marriage and the family can regain its splendor, will the building of the civilization of love truly begin" (13). He also says that "in the newborn child is realized the common good of the family" (11). This means that abortion not only strikes at the child but at the family—and through the family, at society itself.

Archimedes, the ancient Greek scientist, once claimed that if he had a fulcrum and a long enough lever, he could move the world. Children and families are not levers. They're human beings. They're subjects, not objects. Yet Archimedes' words still have value. Families can move the world. The formation that spouses give to each other and to their children—if done with love, courage, energy, and persistence—can move the world and change society.

Let's reflect on just a few specific things you can teach within your families to help that happen.

First, *what you do is more important than what you say.* The greatest gift a father can give his children is to love their mother. Of course, the same applies to wives loving their husbands. Personal example is the most powerful teacher in the world. Your children see everything. If you love each other, they see and learn love. If you love God, they see and learn faith. If you skip Mass, criticize priests, and disagree with the Church on one issue or another, they see and learn that, too.

At the same time, remember that *what you say* is also important. Parents should actively talk about television, newspapers, magazines, books, radio, music, and movies with their children, and explain and correct their content where necessary—because all of these things teach our children. We need to supply the insights that will help our children to reason and understand the moral life. Your children desperately need to know what you think about the world.

Second, *teach your children to seek real freedom, not a counterfeit.* A wider selection of minivans is not freedom. A license to kill unborn children is not freedom. "Choice" is not an end in itself. In fact, when it becomes its own excuse, choice becomes a form of idolatry. Some choices serve the truth about the human person, and therefore serve human dignity. Some choices don't, and therefore attack human dignity. In John's Gospel, Jesus says, "You will know the truth and *the truth will make you free*" (John 8:32; emphasis added). Truth is the inner structure of freedom. Truth and freedom can't be separated. The more we debase the meaning of words like "freedom" to sell cars and computers and cell phones and abortion and assisted suicide, the more we debase ourselves.

Third, *teach your children to seek wisdom, not just knowledge.* Peter Drucker, the American management guru, once wrote that the United States is the first real "knowledge society" in history. What he meant is this. Today, the real wealth and power of a country depend not on armies but on information. In other words, they depend on knowledge. What Francis Bacon wrote five hundred years ago—that "knowledge is power"—has come true with a vengeance in our lifetimes. As a result, our culture has become more and more obsessed with efficiency, productivity, and competition, and we have begun to turn ourselves, and other people, into tools. The most important thing about knowledge is how we choose to use it. That requires wisdom. Fools with tools are still fools. Vatican II warned us that "the future of the world stands in peril unless wiser people are forthcoming" (*GS,* 15). Put wisdom first in the hearts of your children, so that knowledge serves humanity, and not the other way around.

Fourth, *teach your children to see clearly and think critically.* Help them to understand marketing, advertising, and propaganda for what they are—not necessarily "bad" things, but very powerful influences on the way we think and act. The genius of a movie like *The Cider House Rules* is how well it markets something evil as something good.

Fifth, *help your children to remember their own history.* The Catholic faith has a rich and marvelous history, and it's always under attack from people who want to reinterpret the papacy, or the Crusades, or Jesus Himself, to "prove" that the Church is a fraud. Help your children know who they are by teaching them their real Catholic heritage. A community without a sense of history is like a person with amnesia. The past gives meaning to the present, and the present determines the future. This is why the enemies of religious faith always begin by trying to rewrite the history books. Memory is priceless. The genius of the Jewish people is their reverence for memory. Ehud Barak, prime minister of Israel, greeted Pope John Paul II in the Holy

Land in 2000 by saying, "Your Holiness, mine is a nation that remembers ... because without memory there can be neither *culture nor conscience.*"

Sixth, *teach your children to develop the virtues of the heart.* Help them to value *fidelity* instead of broken promises; *patience* instead of restlessness; *simplicity* in place of confusion; *humility* instead of pride; *courage* in place of cowardice; *honesty* instead of excuses; *forgiveness* in place of revenge; *a hunger for justice* in place of apathy.

Seventh, *teach your children to revere the sanctity of life.* Reverence for life is the glue of human community. We can't kill unborn children by the millions or piously help sick people to kill themselves and then expect our young people to create a culture of life. That's why the killings at Columbine High School—as terrible and tragic as they were—made a twisted kind of sense. We've created the environment where Columbines can happen, and we've done it by our own self-absorption and callousness.

Eighth, *teach your children to live 1 Corinthians 13: "Faith, hope and love abide, these three; but the greatest of these is love."* Teach your children how to really love. Ask yourselves why, after twenty centuries, an instrument of execution—the cross—is still the world's greatest symbol of hope. Scripture says that no greater love than this exists: that a man lays down his life for his friends. If we really want to be free, we need to love as Jesus did, in a self-sacrificing way.

Read the Gospel of John again: "You will know the truth, and the truth will make you free." The truth is not an ideology or a product. It's a person. Jesus said, "I am the way, the truth and the life" (Jn 14:6). He also said, "pick up [your] cross and follow me" (Mt 16:24), because the road doesn't end at Golgotha. It ends in Easter and in life. "I am the resurrection and the life" (Jn 11:25). You and your children were made for freedom and for life, so teach them to love well and to choose well, remembering the words of Deuteronomy: "Choose life that you and your descendants may live" (30:19).

Sometimes the headlines in our newspapers tempt us sorely to lose faith in the basic goodness of people. Yet that's a mistake. So very much remains in our country that is decent and honorable. I've always thought of America as that rich young man in Scripture who asks Jesus, "What must I do to have eternal life?" You remember the story. (see Mark 10:17-22). He's a good young man. He has tried to live by the Commandments and to walk in righteousness. Jesus loves and respects him, so He invites the young man to sell what he has and "come follow me." Yet that's too much to ask. The rich young man goes away sad, because he has many possessions, and he can't quite part with them.

Despite all our material advantages, we Americans live in a society saturated by the message that we don't have enough *things;* that we need more *things,* that we deserve more *things,* and that we should get the *things* we want, right now. This is a recipe for sadness. Learn the habit of gratitude, and teach it to your children. What we have is so much more than what we don't have. Gratitude unlocks joy.

This may be why we've had so little joy even within the Church for the last thirty years. We've done a great job over the last three decades arguing about what's supposed to be wrong with the Church and her teaching. Yet we've done a pretty poor job of being grateful for the Church as God's gift to us—a mother who guides us, corrects us, and comforts us out of love, for the sake of our own salvation.

Gratitude unlocks joy. That is why Scripture is filled with praise and thanks to the Lord—from beginning to end:

> Give thanks to the Lord, for He is good,
>   for His mercy endures forever....
> Open to me the gates of justice;
> I will enter them and give thanks to the Lord.
> This gate is the Lord's;
>   the just shall enter it.
> I will give thanks to you, for you have answered me
>   and have been my savior.
>
> PSALM 118:1; 19–21

This is the song of joy meant for every human heart. The family is the school God created to teach it. Teach your children well.

CHAPTER TEN

Not a Burden, but a Joy

No discussion of Catholic married life can avoid some thoughts on one of the most difficult issues of all.

In July 1968, Pope Paul VI issued his encyclical letter *Humanae Vitae* (*Of Human Life*). In it, he reaffirmed traditional Church teaching on the regulation of births. It's certainly the most misunderstood papal statement in recent memory. It led to three decades of doubt and dissent among Catholics throughout the United States. Yet with the passage of time, I believe it has proven prophetic. In fact, I believe it isn't a burden but a joy, and it offers Catholic couples a key to deeper, richer marriages. Let me explain.

Sooner or later, every pastor tries to help someone struggling with an addiction. Usually the problem is alcohol or drugs, and usually the scenario is the same. The addict will admit the problem but claim to be powerless against it. Alternatively, the addict will deny having any problem at all, even if the addiction is destroying his or her health and wrecking job and family. No matter how much sense the pastor makes, no matter how persuasive his arguments, and no matter how life-threatening the situation, the addict simply cannot understand—or cannot act on—the counsel. The addiction, like a thick pane of glass, separates the addict from anything that might help.

One way to understand the history of *Humanae Vitae* is to review the past three decades through this metaphor of addiction. Americans find this teaching so hard to accept not because of any defect in Paul VI's reasoning, but because of the addictions and contradictions we have inflicted upon ourselves, exactly as the Holy Father warned.

In presenting his thoughts, Paul VI warned against four main problems (*HV* 17) that would arise if Church teaching on the regulation of births were ignored. First, he said that the widespread use of contraception would lead to "conjugal infidelity and the general lowering of morality." Exactly this has happened. Few would deny that the rates of abortion, divorce, family breakdown, wife and child abuse, venereal disease, and out-of-wedlock births have all greatly increased since the mid-1960s. Obviously, the birth-control pill hasn't been the only reason. Yet it has played a big role. In fact, the cultural revolution since 1968 would not have been possible without easy access to reliable contraception. In this, Paul VI was right.

Second, he warned that man would lose respect for woman and "no longer [care] for her physical and psychological equilibrium." Man would consider woman "as a mere instrument of selfish enjoyment, and no longer as his respected and beloved companion." In other words, contraception might be marketed as liberating for women, but the real "beneficiaries" of birth control would be men. Three decades later, exactly as Paul VI warned, contraception has largely released males from responsibility for their sexual behavior. Ironically, while many feminists have attacked the Catholic Church for her alleged disregard of women, the Church in *Humanae Vitae* rejected sexual exploitation of women *years before that message entered the cultural mainstream.* Again, Paul VI was right.

Third, the Holy Father warned that widespread use of contraception would place a "dangerous weapon ... in the hands of those public authorities who take no heed of moral exigencies." As we've since discovered, eugenics didn't disappear in 1945. Population control is now a part of nearly every foreign aid discussion. The massive export of contraceptives, abortion, and sterilization by the United States to developing countries— frequently as a prerequisite for aid dollars—is a thinly disguised form of population warfare. Again, Paul VI was right.

Fourth, Pope Paul warned that contraception would mislead human beings into thinking they had unlimited power over their own bodies, turning the human person into an object. Predictably, in the name of the "freedom" provided by contraception and abortion, an exaggerated feminism has undermined the humanity of women. A man and a woman take part uniquely in the glory of God by their ability to create together new life with Him. At the heart of contraception, however, is the idea that fertility is an infection that must be attacked, exactly as antibiotics attack bacteria. Here we can also easily spot the link between contraception and abortion. If fertility can be misrepresented as an infection to be attacked, *so, too, can new life.* In either case, a key element of woman's identity—her potential for bearing new life—is recast as a weakness requiring distrust and "treatment." Woman becomes the object of the tools she relies upon to ensure her own liberation. Man takes no share of the burden. *Once again, Paul VI was right.*

From the Holy Father's final point, a lot has followed: In vitro fertilization, cloning, genetic manipulation, and embryo experimentation can all trace themselves back to contraceptive technology. In fact, we've naively misread the effects of technology not only on society but on our own identity. As Neil Postman once said, technological change is not additive but ecological. A major new technology doesn't "add" something to a society; *it changes everything*—just as a drop of red dye doesn't remain separate in a glass of water. Rather, it colors and changes every single molecule of the liquid. Contraceptive technology, because of its big impact on sexual intimacy, has undermined our understanding of the purpose of sexuality, fertility, and marriage itself. It has scrambled our vocabulary of love, just as pride scrambled the vocabulary of Babel.

U.S. society is more and more often faced with sexual identity problems, family collapse, and a general coarsening of attitudes toward the sanctity of human life. What are we going to do about it? Well, if Paul VI was right about so many of the effects of contraception, *it's because he was right about contraception itself.* So, in seeking to become whole again as persons and as a nation, we need to begin by revisiting *Humanae Vitae* with open hearts. Jesus said the truth would make us free. *Humanae Vitae* is filled with truth. It's therefore one of the keys to our freedom.

One of the problems in communicating the message of *Humanae Vitae* over the last few decades has been the language used in teaching it. The duties of married life are numerous.

They're also serious. They need to be considered prayerfully in advance. Yet few couples understand their love in terms of academic theology. Instead, they *fall in love*. That's the language they use. It's that simple and revealing. They surrender to each other. They give themselves to each other. They *fall into each other* in order to fully possess, and be possessed by, each other. Rightly so. In the sacrament of married love, God intends that spouses should find joy and delight, hope and abundant life, in and through each other—all ordered in a way that draws husband and wife, their children, and all who know them, deeper into God's embrace.

In presenting Christian marriage to a new generation, we need to explain its *fulfilling satisfactions* at least as well as its duties. The Catholic attitude toward sexuality is *anything but* puritanical. God created the human person in His own image. Therefore, the body is good. Catholic marriage—exactly like Jesus Himself—is not about scarcity but abundance. It's not about sterility, but rather the fruitfulness that flows from unitive and procreative love.

Catholic married love *always* implies the possibility of new life. Because it does, it drives out loneliness and affirms the future, and because it affirms the future, it becomes a source of hope in a world prone to despair. In effect, Catholic marriage is attractive because it is true. It's designed for the creatures we are: persons meant for communion. Spouses complete each other. When God joins a woman and man together in marriage, they create with Him a new wholeness; a *"belonging" which is so real, so concrete, that a new life, a child, naturally expresses and seals it*. This is what the Church means when she teaches that

Catholic married love is *both* unitive and procreative—not either/or.

Why can't a married couple simply choose the unitive aspect of marriage and temporarily block its procreative nature? The answer is simple and radical, like the gospel itself. When spouses give themselves entirely to each other, as the nature of married love demands, that *must include their whole selves*—and the most intimate part of each person is his or her fertility. Contraception not only denies this fertility and attacks procreation; in doing so, it damages unity as well. It's the equivalent of spouses saying: "I'll give you all that I am—*except* my fertility; I'll accept all that you are—*except* your fertility." This withholding of self inevitably works to divide the spouses and to damage the holy friendship between them ... maybe not immediately, but deeply, and in the long run often fatally for the marriage.

This is why the Church is not against "artificial" contraception. She's against *all* contraception. *The notion of "artificial" has nothing to do with the issue.* In fact, it tends to confuse things by implying that the debate is about a mechanical intrusion into the body. It isn't. The Church has no problem with science appropriately healing or enhancing bodily health. Rather, the Church teaches that *all contraception is morally wrong;* and not only wrong but seriously wrong. The covenant that husband and wife enter at marriage requires that *all* intercourse remain open to new life. This is what becoming "one flesh" means: complete self-giving, just as Christ withheld nothing of Himself from His bride, the Church, by dying for her on the cross. *Any* intentional interference with the procreative nature of inter-course involves spouses' withholding themselves from each other and from God, who is their partner in sacramental love. In effect, they steal something precious—themselves—from each other and from their Creator.

This is why natural family planning (NFP) differs radically from contraception as a means of regulating family size. *NFP is not contraception. Rather, it's a method of fertility awareness and appreciation.* It's an entirely different approach to regulating birth. NFP does nothing to attack fertility. It doesn't withhold the gift of oneself from one's spouse. It doesn't block the pro-creative nature of intercourse. The marriage covenant requires that each act of intercourse be fully an act of self-giving, and therefore open to the possibility of new life. Yet when, for good reasons, a husband and wife limit their intercourse to the wife's natural periods of infertility during a month, they are simply observing a cycle that God Himself created. They aren't sub-verting it. Therefore, they are living within the law of God's love.

Of course, many wonderful benefits come from the practice of NFP. The wife preserves herself from chemicals or devices and remains true to her natural cycle. The husband shares in the responsibility for NFP. Both learn a greater degree of self-mastery and a deeper respect for each other. It's true that NFP involves sacrifices and periodic abstinence from intercourse. It can be a difficult road. Yet so can any serious Christian life, whether ordained, consecrated, single, or married. Moreover, the experience of tens of thousands of couples has shown that, when lived prayerfully and unselfishly, NFP enriches marriage and results in greater intimacy—*and greater joy.* In the Old Testament, God told our first parents to be fruitful and multiply (see Gn 1:28). He told us to *choose life* (see Dt 30:19). He sent His Son, Jesus, to bring us life abundantly (see Jn 10:10) and to remind us that His yoke is light (see Mt 11:30). I suspect, therefore, that at the heart of Catholic ambivalence toward *Humanae Vitae* is not a crisis of sexuality, Church authority, or moral relevance, but rather a question of faith: *Do we really believe in God's goodness?*

Many couples already live the message of *Humanae Vitae* in their married lives. Their fidelity to the truth sanctifies their own families and the entire community of faith. Those couples who teach NFP and counsel others in responsible Catholic parenthood deserve special praise. Their work too often goes unnoticed or underappreciated. Yet they're powerful advocates for life in an age of confusion. We also owe our prayers and encouragement to those couples who bear the cross of infertility. In a society often bent on avoiding children, they carry the burden of yearning for children but having none. As a result, they're often tempted to use means to achieve pregnancy that seem innocent but undermine human dignity. A good end can never justify a wrong means. Whether to prevent a pregnancy or to achieve one, all techniques that separate the unitive and procreative dimensions of marriage are always wrong. Procreative techniques that turn embryos into objects and mechanically replace the loving embrace of husband and wife *violate human dignity and treat life as a product*. No matter how good their intentions, these methods reduce human life to material that can be manipulated.

A final point: The issue of contraception is not peripheral but central and serious in a Catholic family's walk with God. If knowingly and freely engaged in, contraception is a grave sin, because it distorts the heart of marriage and breaks apart what God created to be whole. Contraception has also done damage to society at large: initially by driving a huge wedge between love and the procreation of children; and then by driving a wedge between sex and love.

Today we have an opportunity that comes only once in many decades. In 1968, Paul VI told the truth about married love. In doing it, he triggered a struggle within the Church that continues to mark American Catholic life even today. The irony is that the people who dismissed Church teaching in the 1960s, soon discovered that they had subverted their own ability to pass anything along to their children. The result is that the Church now must evangelize a world of their *children's* children—adolescents and young adults raised in moral confusion, often unaware of their own moral heritage, who hunger for meaning, community, and love with real substance.

For all its challenges, this is a tremendous new moment of possibility for the Church. The good news is that the Church today, as in every age, has the answers to fill the God-shaped empty places in people's hearts. May God grant us the *wisdom* to recognize the great treasure that resides in our teaching about married love and human sexuality, the *faith, joy, and perseverance* to live it in our own families—and the *courage* that Paul VI possessed to preach it anew.

CHAPTER ELEVEN

"Make Disciples of All Nations"

Jesus was a male, and He called God His Father. That's how Christians think about God, mainly in masculine terms. God is our Father. Jesus is His Son, the New Adam. He's the king, prophet, priest, and bridegroom. All of these are masculine terms. St. Paul tells us that all of us, both male and female, become sons in the Son, through Baptism. Of course, God isn't literally male. Yet gender language is part of the way God reveals His identity to us, and reveals to us our own identities.

St. Paul also tells us that Christ is the bridegroom, and the Church is His bride. This means that all of us, both male and female, are also the spouse of Christ. The Church is not an "it." The Church is a "she." The Church is feminine. That's one reason why Mary is so important to the Catholic understanding of the world. Mary is the first Christian, the perfect model of the Church, and the perfect model for each of us as individual disciples. We're all called to be Mary. That's as hard for some men to accept as it is for some women to call God "He."

Here's the point. What did Mary do? She said "yes" to the Holy Spirit. In that "yes," the Holy Spirit filled her with new life. The early Church called Mary *theotokos,* which is Greek for "God-bearer." As a creature, she allowed her Creator to act *in* her and accomplish great things *through* her. In giving birth to God's son, Mary gave new life to the whole world. We're called to follow her example, each of us in our own way. Hearing the gospel isn't enough. Talking about our faith isn't enough. We have to do something about it. Each of us, in a personal way, needs to be a kind of *theotokos,* a God-bearer. The seed of faith has to bear fruit in a life of Christian action, a life of personal Christian witness, or else it's just words. Talk is cheap.

That's why the feast of Pentecost is so important. Pentecost is the birthday of the Church. Pentecost is our birthday as a believing people. The Church, like Mary, is about new life. The Holy Spirit filled Mary with new life at the Annunciation, and Mary gave birth to Jesus. The Holy Spirit filled the apostles with new life at Pentecost, and they immediately gave birth to a new era through their preaching and example. God is a God of abundance, not sterility; of confidence, not fear. God relentlessly creates new life through each of us, if we allow Him to do so. We are meant to be fertile. We are meant to bring others to new life in Jesus Christ. The Acts of the Apostles should continue today in the witness of our own lives.

God doesn't need anonymous Christians, Christians who blend in, Christians who don't make waves. We're here to rock the boat. That's what it means to be leaven. The Epistle of James says that faith without works is a dead faith. John Paul II says the same thing with a slightly different twist: Faith that does not become culture is dead faith. By "culture" he means the entire environment of our lives. Our culture reflects who we are and what we value. If we really believe in the lordship of Jesus Christ, it will be obvious in our families, our work, our laws, our art, our music, our architecture—in everything.

Faith should impregnate everything we do. It should bear fruit every day in beauty and new life. That's why God doesn't need "nice" Christians, Christians who are personally opposed to sin, but too polite to do anything about it publicly. Mother Teresa was a good and holy woman, but she was not necessarily "nice." Real discipleship should be loving and generous, just and merciful, honest and wise—but also tough and zealous, and determined to turn the world toward Christ.

When Jesus told us, "Go therefore, and make disciples of all nations" (Mt 28:19), He not only gave us the missionary mandate to convert the world; He also gave us the reason to have confidence in accomplishing it. The last thing He told the apostles before returning to His Father in heaven was, "I am with you always, to the close of the age" (Mt 28:20). In that one simple verse is the key to the life of the Church. The Holy Father explained it this way in his 1986 encyclical *Lord and Giver of Life:*

The new "coming" of Christ, this continuous coming of [the Lord] in order to be with His Apostles [and] with the Church, this "I am with you to the close of the age" ... occurs by the power of the Holy Spirit, who makes it possible for Christ, who has gone away, to come now and forever in a new way.... In [the Eucharist and the other sacraments], Christ, who has gone away in His visible humanity, comes, is present and acts in the Church in such an intimate way as to make it His own body. As such, the Church lives, works and grows "to the close of the age." All this happens through the power of the Holy Spirit (61).

Pentecost is not just the birthday of the Church. It's also the feast day of the Holy Spirit, who set the apostles on fire with zeal in the Upper Room, who opened the minds of the crowd that first heard them preach, and who has guided and renewed the life of the Church for two thousand years. Just as He strengthened and encouraged the first apostles, so, too, He will strengthen and encourage each of us—if we let Him.

We begin to understand our vocation as Christians when we acknowledge that God alone is the "Lord and giver of life," and we are His creatures. We become who we really are—we experience reality most vividly—when we allow the Holy Spirit to transform us and to work through us to renew the face of the earth. Each of us is called to share in God's power to give life. That's the meaning of the prayer we all learned as children: "Come Holy Spirit, fill the hearts of your faithful, and enkindle in us the fire of your love. Send forth your Spirit, and we will be created, and You will renew the face of the earth."

If God wants us to be His cooperators in transforming the world, it's because the world needs to change. The world is good because God created it. Yet the world is also sinful, because we have freely made it that way by our sinful choices and actions. Just as Mary said "yes" to God in humility, the modern world too often says "no" to Him in pride. In saying no to God, the world rejects its true identity. In effect, we deny that we're creatures. We want to be the Creator. We want to be the "lord and giver of life."

How should Christians respond to this? To begin with, we need to understand the "real world" as it really is, the way Vatican II described it in *Gaudium et Spes,* the great *Pastoral Constitution on the Church in the Modern World. Gaudium et Spes* saw the world as a pattern of light and shadow, good and evil. Again, that means we need to be actively involved in the world, for the sake of the world. We need to love the world as it needs to be loved—affirming its accomplishments, respecting its freedom, supporting and cultivating its virtues, and cooperating with all of the good in it. That includes all persons of goodwill, whether they're Christian or not.

Reflect on these opening lines from *Gaudium et Spes:* "The joy and hope, the grief and anguish of the men of our time, especially of those who are poor or afflicted in any way, are the joy and hope, the grief and anguish of the followers of Christ as well. Nothing that is genuinely human fails to find an echo in [the] hearts" of the disciples of Jesus. This is "why Christians cherish a feeling of deep solidarity with the human race and its history" (1). Later in the same text, we read, "Christians can yearn for nothing more ardently than to serve the men of this age with an ever-growing generosity and success" (93).

Gaudium et Spes is the best argument for the dignity of the human person—for economic and social justice, for true peace and development—written in the last one hundred years. It provides us with an "examination of conscience" we can apply to just about every aspect of our lives—our personal choices, our parishes, our business activity, our political leaders, everything:

Do we reverence and defend the dignity of the human person from conception to natural death?

Do we really love our enemies? Do we even try?

Do we teach our children to take responsibility for society, and to participate in building up the common good? Do we teach this by our own good example?

Do we preach, by our actions, the dignity of human labor and the value of human activity? Do we live our lives with a purpose—the purpose of co-creating with God a truly human world, a world shaped by the gospel, a "new heaven and new earth"?

Do we promote the nobility of marriage and the sanctity of the family?

Do we work to ensure that our art, science, technology, music, law, entertainment media—all the elements of our culture—advance the real dignity of women and men?

Do we practice justice in our own social and economic relationships? Do we really try to root out the prejudices in our own hearts? Do we encourage justice in our friends, business associates, and leaders?

Do we take an active hand in the political process? Do we demand that our officials promote the sanctity of the human person? Do we do everything in our power to correct or replace them if they don't?

Finally, do we create in ourselves and in our children a sense of international solidarity? The word "Catholic" means universal. We live most of our lives in our families and parishes. That's where our first priorities should always lie. Yet there is no such thing as a "parochial" Catholic. We are all internationalists. This is why issues like hunger, racism, economic development, the rights of migrant workers, religious persecution, even when they happen on the other side of the world, are happening to our brothers and sisters in the Lord. They thus involve us.

We think too little of ourselves when we assume that we were made for nothing better than the "present arrangement" of things. We should never be slaves to the present arrangement. God put us here to be agents of change. Woody Allen once said that "80 percent of life is just showing up." He's funny. Yet, he's wrong. That's a life 80 percent wasted, because there's so much urgent need in the world crying out to be heard.

There is a Ghanaian proverb that goes like this: "God swats the flies of the cow with no tail." It means that God takes care of the poor, because the poor don't have the power to take care of themselves. That's why the Church has a "preferential option for the poor." If God loves and serves the poor, then how can we do anything less? And if that requires political action, so be it. Archbishop Desmond Tutu once said, "I'm puzzled about which Bible people are reading when they suggest that religion and politics don't mix." The great Protestant theologian, Karl Barth, once said that "To clasp hands in prayer is the beginning of an uprising against the world." Vatican II never said, and never meant, that Christians should let the world go to hell because of some mistaken idea of good manners. *Gaudium et Spes* reminds us that the Church is the universal sacrament of salvation and that "the Church has but one sole purpose—that the kingdom of God may come and the salvation of the human race may be accomplished" (45).

The *Letter to Diognetus,* which was written in the second century, says that the Christian is to the world what the soul is to the body. As the soul is present in every part of the body, while remaining distinct from it, so Christians are found in all cities of the world, but cannot be identified with the world.... They live in the flesh, but they are not governed by the desires of the flesh. They pass their days on earth, but they are citizens of heaven.... It is by the soul, enclosed within the body, that the body is held together, and similarly it is by Christians, detained in the world as in a prison, that the world is held together.

This is what the Gospel of John means in chapter 17, verses 14-19. Jesus prays for a Church in, but not of, the world. He prays not that we be taken out of the world, but that we be guarded from the power of the world. We're to be distinct and recognizable as disciples of Christ.

Scripture calls Satan the "Father of Lies" for a reason. We need to get it into our heads that *the gospel* is the real world, even when again and again in daily life we hear that the Church is old-fashioned, or irrelevant, or inflexible, or unrealistic. These are all lies. An interviewer once asked Mother Teresa, "Why are you so holy?" She answered, "You sound as if holiness is abnormal. To be holy is normal. To be anything else is abnormal."

C.S. Lewis once wrote that "heaven is an acquired taste," but only because we have addicted ourselves to sin and its delusions. What some people call "the real world" is usually just the configuration of all those forces that are organized against God. This is *not* the real world. Yet the devil wants us to think it is.

The devil wants us to believe that the gospel view is an idealistic dream. This is insidious, because it traps us in the status quo of those "powers and principalities" that have the world in a death grip. We therefore constantly need to ask ourselves: *Are we an accommodated Church? Have we assimilated too well?* Socrates warned that we should be wary when people praise us. As Christians, we should be worried when nobody wants to persecute us.

Gaudium et Spes tells us that only through Jesus Christ can men and women find eternal life (10). Yet where do we find Jesus Christ? We find Him in the suffering and wounded. In *The Odyssey* (*Book XIX*), when Odysseus finally returns home to Ithaca after years of wandering, he disguises himself as an old man. Not even his wife or son recognizes him. That night, just before bed, the aged nurse who cared for Odysseus in his youth bathes him. She recognizes a scar on his leg. She didn't recognize him *until she saw his scar.* Read the Gospel of John, chapter 20, verses 19-31. The Risen Christ appears to His frightened disciples, and they recognize Him *in seeing His scars.* The Risen Christ has scars. Thus, if you want to see the Risen Christ today, begin by looking for Him in the people who have His scars—the homeless person, the AIDS patient, the mentally handicapped child. The First Letter of Peter says, "By His wounds you have been healed" (2:24). The suffering among us are not some kind of embarrassing mistake. They are Christ's invitation to each of us to *really* live, to *really* believe. We find Him by serving them. Even the apostle Thomas really believed only when he placed his fingers in Jesus' wounds. We need to do the same.

In the early centuries of the Church, one of the great heresies was called Docetism. Docetism was the belief that since Christ was divine, He couldn't really suffer. He only appeared to suffer. Like most great heresies, it seemed to make some sense on the surface. Yet it led to "overspiritualizing" Jesus and turning Him into a kind of idea disconnected from physical reality. That's false teaching, and the Church rejected it. The body and physical suffering are intimately connected to Christ's mission of redemption, so Christians must really be involved in the suffering world, or we're spiritual Docetists.

Our commitment to the suffering world reminds us that justice needs to be at the heart of all our evangelization efforts. The Canadian Indian, Chief Dan George, once said that "When the white man came, we had the land and they had the Bibles. Now they have the land, and we have the Bibles." There's no gospel life without a foundation in justice. We cannot evangelize without doing justice.

"Go, make disciples of all nations" was the last command Jesus gave to us before returning to His Father. It's a big one. How can simple people like us convert the world? That brings us back to Mary, and to the apostles at Pentecost. They changed the world by letting God change them and work through them. We don't need to be afraid. We need to be confident in the promise made by Christ Himself: "I am with you always, to the close of the age."

Don't be afraid of the world. The poet Percy Bysshe Shelley once sneered that "I could believe in Christ if He did not drag along behind Him that leprous bride of His, the Church." Yet Shelley is long dead, and the Church is still here, still alive and young, still bringing life to the world. *Don't be afraid of the world.* The Holy Spirit is on your side. Charles Spurgeon once said, "The way you defend the Bible is the same way you defend a lion. You just let it loose."

So much of the world is already dead without knowing it. That's exactly why people respond to the truth when they hear it. Robert Farrar Capon once wrote, "Jesus came to raise the dead. The only qualification for the gift of the Gospel is to be dead. You don't have to be smart. You don't have to be good. You don't have to be wise. You don't have to be wonderful. You just have to be dead. That's it." So we pray to God to loose the Holy Spirit on the world again in our time, and in our lives, to bring new life to those dead from sin:

Come, Holy Spirit, fill the hearts of your faithful, and enkindle in them the fire of your love. Send forth your Spirit, and we will be created, and you will renew the face of the earth.

Understand the purpose of your life. C.S. Lewis once said that "Christianity, if false, is of no importance; and if true, of infinite importance. The one thing it cannot be is moderately important." So, *away with "moderate" love for the gospel; away with "moderate" love for Jesus Christ.* Time is too limited, too valuable, too important. At the end of every day we need to ask ourselves this simple question: I have paid one day of my life to do what I did today. *Was it worth it?*

At the end of Good Friday, Jesus Christ could say "yes."

How will we answer today?